MY BROTHER ELVIS

THE FINAL YEARS

David E. Stanley

With Paula Phelps

Impello Entertainment
San Diego, CA

Impello Entertainment
info@impelloentertainment.com

Printed in the United States of America First Edition Printing 2016

Editor
Nikki Edwards

Cover Design
Wesley Bryant

Manufactured in the United States of America

ISBN 978-0-9966667-3-2

Also by David E. Stanley

Restoring My Father's Honor: A Son's Crusade
Conversations With The King: Journal of a Young Apprentice
Raised On Rock: Growing Up at Graceland
The Elvis Encyclopedia

For My Brothers
Billy, Ricky and Elvis
And to all who have suffered the effects of drug addiction

Preface

Forty years ago I was a coke head, gun-toting wild child traveling with my stepbrother Elvis Presley as his personal aide and bodyguard. My bond with him began when he took me into his life in 1960 as his youngest stepbrother. Though twenty years his junior, Elvis welcomed me and my siblings with open arms, loving us and caring for us as if we were blood.

Because of this bond I was fiercly loyal to Elvis, and still am to this day.

That is why I decided to tell this story—a story of love, compassion, addiction and devotion. Through the pages of this book, it is my desire to help those dealing with addiction, so that these revelations might save them from the pain I suffered during the final years of Elvis's life. It's my way of reaching out to those that loved Elvis in the hopes of touching their lives as much as Elvis touched mine.

Introduction

It was the summer of 1972 in Memphis, the last day of school for most high school ninth graders. But for 16-year-old David Stanley, school was out forever. The very next day, David was on a private jet heading for New York City, shooting like a rocket into the stratosphere of Rock 'n' Roll superstardom. David would spend the next five years battling the perils of life on the road alongside his stepbrother, Elvis Presley, earning a spot inside a circle few would ever see, and carving himself a place in history as the youngest bodyguard in Rock 'n' Roll history.

My Brother Elvis: The Final Years is David Stanley's story of his beloved brother, his heart wrenching account of Elvis' last 5 years. The book follows David's ascent into manhood, and the struggles of life as the King's brash and unwaveringly loyal bodyguard during the last tumultuous years of Elvis' life. David's whirlwind lifestyle began when he was driven through the gates of Graceland at only four years old. His mother, Dee, had left David's father, Sgt. William "Bill" Stanley, a decorated war hero, to marry Vernon Presley, the father of the legendary singer.

David found himself welcomed into rock's first family by the man who would become both brother and father figure, Elvis Aaron Presley. But he would soon learn that being Elvis' little brother had its downside when he began having difficulties getting along with others in school. When the offer from the King came to become his personal aide and bodyguard, David jumped at the chance. By the tender age of 17, David became an expert in kenpo karate, carrying a nine-millimeter handgun, and most importantly, had the trust of the King.

Life on the road was both a blessing and a curse. David quickly fell into the lavish Rock 'n' Roll lifestyle – plush private jets, unquestioned power, an endless supply of money and drugs, and the company of beautiful women.

In addition to battling his own demons, demons that were fed by life on the road, David also witnessed the problems that would lead to his stepbrother's untimely end. In spite of the eventual insurmountable obstacles, David would become one of Elvis's most trusted allies, brother and bodyguard, fixer and confidant. Through the laughter and tears of the last five years of Elvis' life, David would be there every step of the way, protecting Elvis from everything, except his own worst enemy, himself.

Contents

Graceland

Fate, not bloodlines or choice, made me a part of Rock 'n' Roll's First Family. My mother had left my father, Sgt. William J. Stanley, to marry Vernon Presley, whom she met in Germany, where Elvis was stationed at the time.

In Febuary, 1960, Vernon moved my mom and my two brothers, Billy and Ricky, and me into Elvis's home in Memphis, Tennessee.

Pulling up outside of Graceland for the first time was nothing short of breathtaking. My four year old eyes couldn't seem to open wide enough to take it all in.

Nothing about my early days as the son of a decorated military hero could have predicted that I would eventually end up living here.

My father had been swept out of my life, and I was too young to understand at the time how or why it had happened.

But I did know then that my life would never be the same from that moment forward.

Soon after I met Elvis, who had just returned home from Germany. I had no idea who he was, and I was far too young to have the vaguest concept of what a rock star was. He was a commanding, handsome man, and the charisma that had made him larger than life drew me to him as well. From the moment he first picked me up, I felt from him what I had been craving from my own father. Although I would eventually call Vernon "Daddy", it was Elvis who provided the kind of father figure replacement I had been looking for ever since I had been separated from my father.

It was an uncomfortable situation for Elvis, as he found himself returning from his military duty to discover a completely different world. When he had last lived in this house, his mother was alive, and now she was gone, and Vernon's soon to be new wife – and three young sons – lived there in her stead. He realized that my brothers and I had no more choice in this situation than he did, so he chose to accept us as part of his family rather than distancing himself from us.

Elvis soon left to do the Frank Sinatra show in Miami, and we resumed our new life at Graceland. In June of that year, my father showed up at Graceland to work out the final details of the divorce my Mother had demanded.

My dad knew that Vernon and Mom had him over a barrel; they used us boys as the negotiating chips in a game that had become dramatically lopsided in Mom's favor. We were really the only thing Dad had left to lose, and as the attorneys flanked my mother and Vernon, they explained to him that he would never see his boys again until he signed the divorce papers. Broken and defeated, he signed the papers, collected $2,000 and a Cadillac from Vernon, then hugged us goodbye. His heart was breaking as he promised that he would always love and take care of us. For all the military battles he'd fought and won, the one that meant the most to him was simply bigger than he was. Wiping tears from his eyes, he walked out the door.

I had no way of knowing any of this at the time of course, as I was too young to be privy to the details. All I knew was that my father had disappeared. Out of longing, I replaced him with Elvis, who was half big brother, half father figure. But life was not a fairy tale, despite outward appearances. I wrestled with the complications of the clubfoot I had struggled with since birth, and continued wearing braces until I was about six or seven years old. This only added to the stares as I was already big for my age. It was an interesting world of contrasts that I lived in; on the one hand, I had experienced incredible physical pain and deformity, yet on the other, I lived a life that others envied. Unbeknownst to me at that time, I was part of rock 'n' roll royalty, and the simple life I'd been born into had given way to one of power, prestige and privilege.

Despites all the vestiges of wealth that surrounded me, and regardless of the fact that I had everything a boy could dream of, I knew from an early age that something was amiss. I could feel deep within my bones that something terrible had happened in my family, though I couldn't voice my feelings or even completely understand them. This sense of loss or injustice created a burning anger within me, one that couldn't be abated by the constant prayers of my mother or the strict religious upbringing she adhered to. I was too young to understand how to express these feelings, and it wouldn't take long for that anger to bubble to the surface and spill over.

The cocoon of my comfortable life at Graceland changed the day that I started going to school. By then, we had moved to a new house built for our family. My brothers, Billy and Ricky, were already in school, so everyone already knew who we were. While they seemingly adjusted well to life in public school, my transition didn't come nearly as easily. I had a fiery temper and a short fuse, and these outbursts resulted in being held back and repeating first grade. Now, instead of just being a big, disabled kid with a famous stepbrother, I was an angry big kid who had to repeat first grade. It made me an easy target for the bullies at school, and only added fuel to the fire that raged within me.

My mother's strict religious upbringing kept her convinced that the difficulties with her children were a direct result of her own sin. She insisted on attending frequent church services, and every time the church doors opened, the Stanley boys were there. We attended Sunday morning services, Sunday night services, Wednesday night prayer meetings, vacation bible school, church camp, revival meetings – you name it, we were there. Each night, my mother joined us for our prayers, but all the prayers in the world couldn't quell the anger that continued rising inside of me. I had no one to talk to and no way of coming to grips with my anger alone.

I made it to the fourth grade before the rage boiled over far enough to warrant serious consequences—I was kicked out of school. A boy was making fun of me, and when he ignored my threats to stop or else, I hit him. A teacher who witnessed it came over and grabbed me, so I hit him too. It was the first of many physical altercations with authority figures that were to come. Though I was suspended, I really didn't care. I hated school and was mad as hell, so anyone who messed with me was going to pay the price.

As much as I loved this life at Graceland, it still confused me. I wondered what had happened to my dad, and why Vernon had replaced him so suddenly. On the occasions when I tried talking to my mom about it, she would dismiss my questions with the explanation that my father was nothing but a drunken brawler. Something told me her explanation was lacking, but in my young mind I had no way to verbalize that. So I stuffed those uneasy feelings deep inside of me, letting them further ignite my inner rage.

I was growing into a big kid, and I longed to play sports. The limp created by the nearly two-dozen surgeries in my early years lingered into grade school, but I discovered that I was still able to excel in football. It became my passion and a much needed outlet for my anger, but that passion was stripped away from me in the fifth grade when I tore the cartilage in my knee. Now sidelined from the one outlet I'd found to release my frustration, my anger began simmering out of control.

This caused me to act out in ways that both frustrated and angered my mom and Vernon. I was about ten years old when some neighborhood boys and I stole a six-pack of beer from the corner store. We were caught of course, and Vernon was so mad about it that he made me drink the whole thing. I was sick as a dog, but it did nothing to instill the lesson he'd set out to teach me as I was too stubborn to accept it.

The difficulties created by my rage led mom to take me out of public school, and by the seventh grade she had enrolled me an exclusive Christian school. I was still big for my age, already almost six feet tall and weighing around one hundred and sixty pounds, and was still unwilling to take direction from anyone.

As I sat in school one day, I absent-mindedly bounced my legs beneath my desk. Because of my size, my knees were hitting the underside of my desk and causing the whole thing to move. Tired of the incessant disruption, my teacher came up and grabbed me by the ear, leading me into the hallway. The short fuse had just been lit, and the second we stepped into the hallway, I hauled off and hit him, dropping him to the floor. I then made a break for the door, and was already in the parking lot before the principal caught up with me and tackled me to the ground. We both made it back up to our feet, and I also dropped him with a single punch. My brother Billy learned of the incident as it was unfolding. A classmate sitting near the window said, "Hey, Billy, isn't that your little shit of a brother out there kicking the principal's ass?"

It was, and my short tenure at that particular school ended immediately.

The more problems my anger created, the more rigid my mother became, and the more I rebelled. Her anger only fueled mine. The next stop after the Christian school was the Castle Heights Military Academy, where psychiatrists tried to get inside my head while the instructors tried to keep me in line. They had clearly met their match, and neither were very successful.

I had become an arrogant, smart-ass, foul mouthed kid, with no respect for authority of any sort in my life. Elvis had started to get concerned, and pulled Vernon aside saying, "Daddy, we need to watch this kid. He's a ticking time bomb waiting to go off." Military school seemed the logical answer, but by the time I'd been there for eight weeks, I could no longer stand it. I had to find a way to escape this, and the only exit door I could find was written in their stringent rulebook.

One of the requirements of the school is that all students had to march and do close order drills every day, no exceptions. If you didn't march, you couldn't attend the academy. Knowing that, one night I took a brick, gritted my teeth and smashed it over the knee that I'd torn up while playing football in the fifth grade.

By the morning, my knee was so swollen that my uniform pants barely fit around it. They called us to march, and I remained seated. When the commanding officer told me I had to march, I smugly showed him my knee. After a visit to the doctor's office, I was discharged from Castle Heights Military Academy. I was too smart for my own good.

Having given up on the private schools, mom enrolled me in White Haven Junior High School in 1967, the same year that Elvis and Priscilla married. I actually managed to complete my junior high years without expulsion – although, of course, not entirely without incident.

I had discovered new outlets for my inner demons, not the least of which was boxing. There was something extremely gratifying about boxing, and my size, strength, and natural athletic ability I had inherited from my father only lent to my success at the sport. By the time I was fifteen, I was obsessed with Golden Gloves boxing and even became the light heavyweight champion in my county. It helped me re-direct some of the intense anger that plagued me, but it seemed that nothing could completely assuage those feelings.

It's Only Rock 'n' Roll, But I Like It

E lvis became increasingly concerned by my often belligerent ways, and took me aside on more than one occasion in an attempt to get through to me.

"I was angry when I was a kid, too," he would tell me. "You need to mellow out."

It wasn't as simple as that. I still wasn't sure why I was so angry, I just knew that I was. As I entered my teen years, I had started realizing that not everyone who befriended me had an interest in me, most times they were just interested in hanging out with Elvis' stepbrother. It made me guarded and cautious, uncertain of who to trust and extremely selective with my friendships.

If there was anything that rivaled the outlet I found through boxing, it was music. Growing up at Graceland, music was obviously a huge part of my life from a very young age. Elvis listened to a lot of gospel music, and he loved the music of Tom Jones, the Imperials, Dottie Rambo and the Statler Brothers. My tastes leaned so far away from his that we were seemingly inhabiting different planets, and it is something we would never see eye-to-eye on.

For me, my love for music began the first time I ever heard The Beatles. Despite Elvis' speculation that they were causing the downfall of the day's youth, I could not get enough of their music. (Interesting perspective on his part considering millions of parents thought the same of his music.) I listened to the Rolling Stones, Grand Funk Railroad, and Three Dog Night. Once I heard The Who, Deep Purple and Black Sabbath, that was it. I'd finally found the music that would become the soundtrack of my life, the tunes that seemed to give perspective to the mass confusion of my world. In the dichotomy of my music, I was able to make sense of my life's chaos. As the song famously said, it was only Rock 'n' Roll, but I liked it.

I started playing drums and joined a series of little garage bands. I had found my running around buddies; guys I trusted and could hang with, just being myself – not Elvis' stepbrother. When I entered Hillcrest High School in 1969, I was finally stepping into my own, becoming your "average" high-school kid. Well, as average as any high-school kid can be when they're the stepbrother of an icon. Elvis began doing live concerts again starting with a 30 day engagement at the International Hotel in Las Vegas. Mom and Vernon took us boys out there so we could attend a few of the shows. Although I had seen Elvis live in a benefit concert in Memphis in 1961, it was in Las Vegas in 1969 that I realized just how big he truly was. Until then, I knew he was a star, but seeing him in his black jump suit stunning the sold-out crowd, defined for me exactly why he was the King of Rock 'n' Roll.

Several months later, on April 17, 1970, I saw Led Zeppelin in concert, and the King of Rock 'n' Roll was quickly and permanently dethroned—at least in my mind. From that moment on, as hard as Elvis would try to steer my musical tastes, my thirst for rock music could neither be quenched or redirected.

The freewheeling times of the 1960's were creating a fast-paced backdrop for my rebellious adolescent adventures. I was smoking pot by the age of 15, which led to one of the more memorable encounters with Elvis that I would have in my young life.

In December of 1970, Elvis had flown to Washington to meet with President Richard Nixon to discuss becoming a "federal agent at large" for the Bureau of Narcotics. Unbeknownst to me, there was such a thing if you were Elvis Presley. It was something of a spur-of-the-moment decision, and while he was gone, Billy and I went out cruising with my buddy Robert Watson. The old saying, when the cat's away the mice will play was definitely ringing true for us boys.

After we'd gotten completely stoned, we went to McDonald's, where I devoured four cheeseburgers, some fries and a couple of milkshakes before we dropped Robert off at his house and returned to Graceland.

When we got back to Graceland, we were surprised to see one of Elvis's life long friends, Lamar Fike, there. He told us that Elvis had just gotten back from Washington. About that time, the phone rang and Lamar picked it up.

"Yeah boss. Will do. I'll send 'em right up."

From the closed-circuit television sets in his room, Elvis had seen us return, and now he wanted to have a talk. My heart dropped into my stomach--I knew we were dead. The pot-induced paranoia added to the feeling of impending doom that I felt the second Lamar had picked up the phone. Billy and I were both trying to hold it together and be cool, but we knew we were probably too stoned to pull it off.

We made our way upstairs to Elvis' office and sat on the couch. I had mustard and assorted bits of McDonald's leftovers clinging to my John Lennon t-shirt, and couldn't seem to wipe the shit eating grin off my face to save my life. Elvis walked into the room, still wearing the white shirt, black pants and cape immortalized to this day in the photo of him and President Nixon.

"Hey, howya doin'?" I asked him, trying to act as normal and nonchalant as I could possibly muster considering my current condition.

Elvis walked directly over to us without saying a word, and with a flourish, flashed a badge that had been hooked onto his belt. He flipped open the black leather case and stuck it in my face.

"Do you know what this is?" he demanded of me.

My only thought was "Oh, shit." The only words on the badge that didn't alarm me were "U.S." The other words – "Bureau of Narcotics" nearly had me wetting my pants.

"Yes sir, I know what it is," I stammered in spite of myself. "Where'd you get it?"

"The President of the United States gave me this, David," he said seriously.

Beyond music was another topic Elvis and I cold not agree upon, politics, and I found myself amused by his grave tone. In fact, the thought of President Nixon handing Elvis an official badge suddenly struck me as being very humorous.

"You mean Dick gave it to you?" I asked, no longer worried about getting busted. Elvis was too wrapped up in the day's events to realize how stoned Billy and I were.

Elvis glared at me.

12

"That's 'President Nixon' to you– do you understand me?" Elvis reprimanded.

"Wow! He gave it to you? You didn't buy it?" I asked cheekily.

"No, goddammit, I didn't buy it. I told you, The President gave it to me."

I could tell Elvis was taking this whole thing quite seriously, and the more serious he became, the more fun I was having with it. Elvis began explaining that he had gone to Washington to volunteer his services to help fight the war on drugs amongst young people. He was obviously annoyed that Billy and I were not nearly as excited about his quest. To his credit, Billy was doing a fine job of keeping his mouth shut through all of this clearly thinking I would hang myself with my own rope.

"That's great," I said, not meaning it and wondering what all of this had to do with Billy and me. Unfortunately, for us, we soon found out.

"I have an assignment for you," Elvis said. "I want you to be the eyes and ears of both myself and the President at Hillcrest High School."

I couldn't believe what I was hearing.

"You want us to be *WHAT*?" I exclaimed in sheer shock.

Elvis measured his words carefully as he delivered them.

"You are on special assignment – by the President of the United States – and I want you to do this."

There was really only one thing for me to say.

"Yes sir," I responded. I wondered if that silly grin was still on my face, because I felt as if I would burst out laughing at any second at the irony of it all.

"You've got the long hair, so you look like a hippie," he explained. "You can do this. I mean it. You're to report to me directly, and I will report directly to the President."

"Of the United States?" Billy asked.

"That's what I said, damn it!" Elvis replied, now becoming visibly frustrated with our notable lack of enthusiasm for his new mission.

Realizing we weren't busted, we started to relax a bit. We somehow managed to keep straight faces as we promised the King that we'd become narcs at our own high school. Satisfied, Elvis dismissed us with a nod.

We made it all the way to the back steps before we both broke out in howls of laughter. We leaned against one another, laughing so hard that tears rolled down our flushed cheeks. As we fought to regain our composure, we suddenly heard gunfire coming from the side of the house. Knowing what it was, we walked around the building to see Elvis in the backyard along with four of five members of his renowned "Memphis Mafia." Elvis was still wearing his black outfit, only now it was accessorized with a fully automatic Thompson submachine gun. As we watched, he fired round after round of ammunition into the silhouettes around the shooting range.

"Billy?" I said.

"Yeah?"

"I think he's serious about this narc shit."

We looked at each other and, once again, fell victim to a fit of laughter.

Billy and I never pulled through for Elvis on that mission. We were definitely by-products of our era, reveling in the rebellion of the day and finding plenty of adventure in drugs and music. Elvis was strictly against street drugs, although he thought his own addictions were acceptable because they came via the prescription pad of a licensed physician.

For my sixteenth birthday in 1971, Vernon gave me my first car, a black 1957 Chevrolet 327 with a red leather interior and mag wheels. Everything in life was going my way. Ricky already was touring with Elvis, working as part of his entourage, and he'd bring back stories from the road that we found almost impossible to believe. The notion that Elvis and the rest of the guys had girlfriends on the road and partied all night was beyond my comprehension as it was a complete contradiction to the conservative man that I had grown up with. The Elvis I knew at home was a solid family man, not a womanizing rock 'n' roller.

I craved the excitement that Ricky's tales of road bespoke. I had just finished my ninth grade year (which should have been my tenth), and Elvis was getting ready to leave for a 15-day tour opening with a two-night stand at Madison Square Garden in New York City.

My time finally came. Elvis called me in his room upstairs at Graceland. As I shut the door behind me he simply asked,

"You wanna go to work for me?"

"Yes," I said.

"Good."

He picked up a small box sitting on a table next to him and opened it. I could see the infamous TCB emblem and lighting bolt at the end of a chain. It was the embodiment of Elvis' slogan, "Taking Care of Business in a Flash," and in the King's world, this was the equivalent of being knighted. As he placed it around my neck he said,

"We're leaving tomorrow David. You're going with us."

It was my mother's worst nightmare come to fruition. The family that she had fought so hard to keep together was flying the coop. She had already lost Ricky to life on the road, and now she was losing me too. But there was nothing she could do to keep me from going. I was ready to break free, and Elvis had just handed me a one-way ticket to freedom.

Let Me Go Rock 'n' Roll

I was packing the following morning when my mom came into my room. The look in her eyes told me that she had heard the news, but we both knew that there would be no way of stopping me now. It felt as if I had been waiting my entire life for this opportunity; it was the rite of passage I had dreamed of from the moment I discovered music. Being a part of Elvis' family was one thing; becoming a part of his entourage was something entirely different. I was entering into an elite inner circle that could only be accessed with the blessing of the King himself.

She entered my room slowly, as if she was still clinging to the hope that what she'd heard around the house wasn't true. As mom's eyes landed on the gleaming "TCB" necklace around my neck, it confirmed that everything she had heard was true.

"Oh, hey, Mom."

"Where are you goin' David?"

Our eyes met and I could see that she was terrified of the answer.

"Mom, you know where I'm goin'."

She nodded, glancing once again at the suitcase crammed with clothes that was sitting on my bed.

"Yeah, David, I know," she said. "Look, David, I was thinking...maybe it's not such a good idea."

"Don't start, Mom," I said firmly, continuing to pack. Nobody, not even my mother, was going to keep me from this adventure. I had nothing to keep me in Memphis, and there was a whole world out there just waiting for me.

"What about school, son?"

"School's out. This is just for the summer."

"What happens in the fall?"

"We'll deal with that in the fall. Mom, I'm going."

"But you know how important your education is."

"Mom, I'll go back to school. And if I don't, Elvis can get me the best tutors in the world."

In actuality, school was the furthest thing from my mind. All I knew was that I had a plane to catch, and there was no way that it was leaving the ground without me. My mother's face was filled with a combination of concern and fear, and she struggled to find the argument that would make me change my mind.

"But, David – David, you're only sixteen years old," she exclaimed.

"I'll be fine, Mom," I said with a heavy sigh. "You know the guys, they'll all watch out for me."

"What about church, David? You know Jesus Christ and rock 'n' roll don't mix."

"Spare me, Mom."

"We need to discuss this, David."

"There's nothing to discuss!"

She was crestfallen, realizing that there was no changing my mind at this point.

"Oh, David, I'm losing you too."

"Don't talk like that! It's just a tour, Mom. I'll be back before you can even start to miss me."

I walked over and wrapped my arms around her petite frame. She returned the hug, clinging to me like a life raft.

"David, I am so sorry..." she began and I pulled away, putting her at arms' length and looking down into her face. Tears dampened her eyes and she looked grief-stricken.

"What? Sorry? Sorry for what?"

She shook her head, the lump in her throat making it difficult to speak.

"I'm not..." she paused, visibly struggling for the right words to say as I stood there, completely puzzled.

"Son, I've done things in my life that I'm not very proud of. Lord knows I've made my share of mistakes. But everything I've done – right or wrong – I was doing it for you boys. I hope you don't hate me for that."

"What are you talking about? I don't hate you for anything. But you know what? You made your choices, and I have to make mine."

The tears that moistened her eyes began slipping down her cheeks, and I turned to zip up my suitcase, not wanting to delve any deeper into the emotion of the moment. She stood in my room, silently watching me, as I tried pretending I didn't feel her gaze boring into my back. When she spoke, her voice was shaky.

"I'll pray for you, son."

"I know you will, Mom. I know you will."

She paused for a moment as if she had something else to say, but instead turned and walked from my room. I knew that she worried about what happened on the road, but she also knew there was no way of keeping it away from me. Her husband and middle son were already part of Elvis' entourage, and there was absolutely no way that she could take that family tradition away from me.

The limousines took us from Graceland to the private area of the airport, where a gleaming BAC 111 was waiting. I had flown on private planes with Elvis before, but this was different. There was an electric feeling in the air, an excitement and buoyancy that wasn't unlike the last day of school. The men I'd known all of my life now seemed more like fraternity brothers, and it was obvious that they were ready to cut loose and have a good time.

I took my seat on one of the plane's plush sofas and let my eyes drink in the world around me. Elvis and his current girlfriend, Lisa, had retreated to his room at the back of the plane, and the men were settling in to play cards and enjoy a beer together.

All of the faces were ones I'd known forever. Red and Sonny West – cousins who were Elvis' main bodyguards – had become fixtures around Graceland. Elvis' tour manager Joe Esposito, his music coordinator Charlie Hodge, security chief Dick Grob, bodyguard Jerry Schilling and Elvis' best friend, Lamar Fike, all were familiar faces to me. James Colley – a man we knew as "Hamburger James" because his chief duty seemed to be going out and picking up hamburgers – was there as well. GeeGee Gambill, who was married to Elvis' cousin, Patsy, and my brother Ricky were there as Elvis' personal assistants.

As I sat silently looking at the world I had been thrust into, Lamar joined me on the couch.

"How ya doin', David?"

"This is so cool!"

He smiled in a kind of fatherly way, then took on a bit more serious tone.

"You know, David, things are different on the road," he began. I looked at him and nodded, realizing that we were about to have some sort of important conversation.

Lamar began explaining to me in a kind, but firm tone that I had become part of something that most people would never have the opportunity to experience. But, he reminded me, this opportunity carried with it responsibilities that could never be ignored.

"Things happen, David. And it stays between us. You leave it behind when you leave the plane. You don't bring the road home with you."

I nodded, understanding the gist of the conversation but not fully grasping the magnitude of what he was saying. Ricky had talked to me about the hordes of screaming girls we would encounter on the road, but there was simply no way to understand the kind of access I now had to a world that was beyond my comprehension. There would no longer be anyone who would refuse me anything. The guys would all have a similar discussion with me over the next few days, and by the end of the tour, the message was loud and clear. This wasn't the life we knew at Graceland, and what happened on the road was meant to stay there.

As I looked around, I noticed that many of the men had slipped off their wedding rings. Black books came out, and conversations began taking a raunchy turn. Before my very eyes, I watched as the men who had helped shape my views of the world and teach me right from wrong now morph into something unrecognizable. These were men whose wives I knew, whose kids I had grown up with. I had admired them, wanted to be like them. Now I wasn't sure exactly who they were, but I was sure as hell curious to find out.

My alternative education had officially begun. I was about to become a confused boy in a man's world, not certain which truths were actually true. The rules had changed the instant the door of the plane clicked closed.

I knew why most of the men were on the plane; the only one whose presence puzzled me was George Nichopolus, or Dr. Nick as he was known, who was Elvis' so-called personal physician. It seemed odd to me that Elvis, who was in peak physical condition, would need his doctor to travel with him on the tour.

"Hey, Lamar, what's the doc doin' here?" I inquired.

"He goes on every tour," Lamar responded, avoiding the answer.

"Why?"

"Tell you what. Why don't we go to the back and see the Boss?" Lamar suggested, knowing that he had set the stage for what Elvis had to say.

"Boss?" I asked confused.

Lamar smiled. "That's right. He's Boss now."

That was fine with me. I'd call him whatever he wanted for the chance to be out on the road. I made my way to the back of the plane and was stunned to see the elaborate bedroom. Even for Elvis it seemed extravagant. I gave a low whistle as I looked around, and Elvis chuckled at my wide-eyed amazement.

"How ya doin', David? The guys treatin' you okay?"

I nodded as I looked around.

"Yeah, great. This is great! You've even got your own bedroom?!"

Elvis gave the laugh that made women swoon.

"Yeah, pretty crazy, huh?" he said sheepishly.

He and Joe exchanged a glance and Joe excused himself from the room. Lisa sat on the arm of Elvis' chair and silence filled the air for a brief moment.

"Listen, David, I wanted to tell you how glad I am to have you on tour," he said. "I see a lot of potential in you, David. I want you to watch and learn; I'm grooming you to become my bodyguard one day."

In a day that already had been a dream come true, his words resonated through me and filled me with an excitement that went beyond words. I wasn't sure exactly why Elvis needed a bodyguard, but I knew I was up to the task.

"You know my dad was a bodyguard," I volunteered eagerly, wanting to reinforce the wisdom of his plan. He smiled.

"I know that," he said. "You're a lot like your father, David."

"I didn't know him that well."

"Well, I did, David. He's a good man. You're a lot like him – you're big, just like him – but you're also very aggressive. You have a very strong nature."

I nodded. My problems in school were no secret. I was a hotheaded kid who used size to my advantage and defy to authority. Somehow, Elvis had seen the potential in all of that. He knew that I had to fight my way out of situations that came as a direct result of being his little brother and walking with a limp, and he sympathized with what it was like to be misunderstood.

"I know things haven't worked out well for you in school, and you bottle up a lot of anger," he continued. "I want to channel that. I want you to stay close to Red and Sonny. They'll watch out for you and you can learn a lot from them. It can get pretty ugly out there. Understand?"

"Yes sir!"

"When we get to L.A., I'm going to introduce you to Ed Parker. I think he can do a lot for you."

"Who's that?"

I might as well have asked someone on the street who Elvis Presley was. Elvis looked at me for a moment, then launched into Ed's impressive history. Senior Grandmaster Ed Parker, I quickly learned, was to Kenpo Karate what Elvis was to Rock 'n' Roll. Known as the Father of American Kenpo, he was a martial arts pioneer, and one of Elvis' dear friends and personal karate instructor. As Elvis explained to me who Ed was, and why he wanted me to work with him, I could feel my excitement growing. High school and Memphis seemed a million miles away, and I knew I had finally found the place where I belonged.

Whole Lotta Love

We landed in New York and a bus pulled alongside our plane. While Ricky and GeeGee began transferring the luggage from the plane into the bus, Elvis motioned for me to join him in the waiting limousine.

"I promised your mother I'd take care of ya," he explained as I slid into the car along with Lisa, Vernon, Red, Sonny, James and Joe. The rest of the guys would take the bus to the hotel. It was my first trip to New York, and I was silent as I looked in amazement at the skyscrapers surrounding us.

"Hey, Elvis, isn't that the Entire State Building?" James asked.

"What did you say?" Elvis asked incredulously.

"The Entire State Building. Isn't that it?"

We all burst out laughing as James sat dumbfounded, trying to understand what we all found so hilarious. When Elvis finally stopped laughing, he was able to explain that yes, the building we had just passed was in fact the Empire State Building.

We made our way to the Hilton Hotel at the Plaza of Americas where we had the entire top floor to ourselves, with Elvis in the main suite. The band would fly in on its own plane and later help populate the floor below us. Before the night was done, I would learn that hanging out with the band was the way to go; there were always plenty of women flocking around them, hoping to get close to the King, or at least get close to someone who was close to the King.

As the evening progressed, Elvis' suite became filled with band members, his entourage, and, as usual, beautiful women. I was like a kid in a candy store, walking around looking at the bevy of available beauties. Elvis called me over and introduced me to a small group of paid escorts who were there for the night. Each and every one of them was drop-dead gorgeous, and it was obvious that he already had given them a bit of background on me. I didn't know which one I was going to end up with, and it didn't matter – all of them were stunning.

"Ladies, I give you the boy," he told them with a knowing smile. "Now bring me back the man."

Barely believing my good fortune, I watched in disbelief as all five of the women rose to their feet and warmly welcomed me. I tried acting cool as we made our way back to my room, although inside I was jumping up and down like a little kid at Christmas. No, this was *way* better than Christmas. My mom would have skinned Elvis alive had she known.

My nervousness kicked in by the time we got inside my room, and the women – who all were in their mid-twenties – began to make their moves. As I sat on the bed, with women and hands seeming to be everywhere, I was hoping that I would never wake up from this dream. High school was never like this!

"Is this your first time, honey?" the woman beside me whispered into my ear, using her tongue to help propel the words along.

I shook my head nervously, staring at the pair of breasts that now were exposed in front of me.

"D'ya like 'em?" a second woman asked and I nodded, swallowing hard, unable to speak.

"You know," the woman at my side continued as her fingers found my zipper. "Most guys would be riding us hard by now. Whatsamatter? You shy?"

I shook my head and leaned back on the bed to accommodate her roving hands. I could hear the other womens' clothes coming off, could feel hands running everywhere on my body. I closed my eyes as my own shirt was pulled over my head. I had been right about one thing that day, being at Elvis' side had already brought the best tutors in the world.

The first order of business the next day was to head to Elvis' suite for breakfast. It was a two-story penthouse with incredible views of the New York City skyline. I awoke early, ready for my first full day as part of Elvis' inner circle.

Elvis had already finished eating when I arrived, and Ricky and Dick Grob had gotten there before I did. As a personal assistant, part of Ricky's duties included getting up before Elvis, ordering room service and having the spread ready before rousing the King. I entered the suite just in time to see Elvis running at full speed up the spiral staircase. I watched, puzzled, as Dick Grob looked at his stopwatch and shouted out a time.

"What the ..." I began.

"I can beat that," Ricky said with disdain. I watched as Ricky took his position at the bottom of the stairs, then gave a nod to Dick that he was ready.

"Go!" Dick shouted, starting the clock as Ricky shot up the stairs as fast as he could.

Within moments, I was joining them in their game, racing up and down the spiral staircase as we worked to beat one another's best time. I would soon discover that there were countless activities that we would create to pass time on the road. It was our way of killing time and breaking up the tension that comes from sitting around and waiting.

Elvis's manager, Colonel Tom Parker, who was something of a rare presence in our midst, interrupted our friendly competition. Although I had known him for as long as I could recall, his demeanor was entirely different when it came to work. I discovered that the same man who had gifted me stuffed animals and toys when I was a child, someone whom I had known as a friendly uncle, now barely acknowledged my presence. Unless he had a reason to discuss business, he simply didn't interact with us on the road.

"Listen, we need to get ready – we've got a press conference in an hour," he announced.

The lighthearted ambience we had been enjoying disappeared as soon as the words left the Colonel's mouth. The room suddenly became all business. Within the hour we were whisked into the hotel's ballroom, which had been transformed into a media center. With cameras rolling and flashbulbs popping, the press questioned Elvis on everything from his longevity as an artist, to current events, to his politcal views.

One of the questions he fielded early on during the press conference referred to Elvis' humble beginnings as a poor, shy country boy. He rose to his feet, showing off his lean, tan frame bedecked in a trim blue suit with a huge gold belt buckle. Giving his famous crooked grin, Elvis replied, "I don't know, I don't think I look too shy – you tell me..."

I realized then the extent of his charm. In a room full of New York journalists trying to find a chink in his armor, he managed to be both entirely confident and a bit self-deprecating. Persistent and determined to find a juicy tidbit that could be used in a headline, the media then pressed him to give his stance on the Vietnam War.

"I'd just as soon not comment on that," Elvis replied.

A journalist asked him if he thought all celebrities should refuse to take a political stance.

"No, ma'am, I can't speak for all the rest, I'm just speaking for me," he said with his signature southern drawl.

I watched in fascination as the journalists grew more intense and urgent in their questions. Elvis seemed completely at ease behind the microphone, as casual as if he was back in his luxurious bedroom on the private plane.

"Tell me about the image, the King," another reporter demanded.

"The image is one thing, the person's another," Elvis said.

"Is there a difference?" came the reply.

"Oh, yes, ma'am, there certainly is," he said.

I realized that I was just getting to know him. I had known him as the person, not as the King or the superstar that everyone else worshipped. Even though much was written about his humble beginnings and his love for his mother, his generosity and his strong spiritual roots, nobody really knew him. I was meeting Elvis the superstar for the first time, and unbeknownst to me, the man I was getting to know bore little resemblance to the stepbrother who had practically raised me.

Once we had completed the press conference and returned to Elvis' suite, our afternoon passed realtively quietly. I could feel the excitement rising as the first show grew closer, but if anyone else felt the same way, it wasn't obvious from their actions. They were aware of the time, and what we had left to do that day, but certainly weren't consumed with it. We hung out in Elvis' suite watching "Match Game '72" on television. It was one of Elvis' favorite shows, so he never missed it, and whatever came on after it usually got viewed by default.

Finally, Joe arrived and said it was time to get ready for the show. I was excited more than I was nervous. GeeGee and Ricky – referred to as "the wrecking crew" – met Elvis in his room with a couple of jumpsuits. Elvis had seen a Dean Martin movie named "The Wrecking Crew" and thought it sounded cool, so he gave the same name to the men who put him together every night. Charlie began fixing Elvis' hair. For the final touch, they slipped Elvis' rings onto his fingers, then began putting Band-aids on his fingers, just below the knuckles of each finger wearing a ring.

"What's that for?" I asked.

"I don't want anyone pulling my rings off," he explained. "This keeps 'em from sliding off my hands."

Once Elvis was dressed, Jerry joined him for some stretching and calisthenics to loosen him up for the stage. The routine ran like clockwork, and though it would later become second nature to me,

I was amazed at the meticulous timing from each member of the crew. Their duties were as choreographed as any dance routine, and each man seemed to know exactly when to step up and perform their assigned task. This was clearly not their first rodeo.

Joe indicated it was time to go, and we walked silently to the service elevator. I was at Elvis' side, just where he had told me to stay. No one spoke as we made our way downward, and when the doors finally opened, we walked onto the hotel's loading dock. Four limousines were already waiting with their engines running.

I followed Elvis into the limo along with Lisa, Vernon, Joe, Red and Sonny. The sights outside our window, coupled with the growing mood of anticipation inside the car, created a sense of uncontrollable excitement. I could feel the energy on both sides of the window, and I knew it was just a taste of what was to come.

We made our way briskly through the backstage area. As we neared Elvis' dressing room, I caught a glimpse of George Harrison. If anyone could outshine Elvis at that moment for a Rock 'n' Roller like me, it would have to be a Beatle.

"Hey! There's George Harrison over there!" I announced excitedly to the rest of the guys. They looked at me, barely blinking and refused to acknowledge the importance of my announcement. While the rest of the crew continued walking, I rushed over to introduce myself to George.

The closest I had come to The Beatles up until that point was in 1966, when Brian Epstein and John Lennon had shown up at our house adjacent to Graceland, looking for Elvis. While the rest of the band waited in the car, John and Brian Epstein were facing down my mother, who wasn't about to let them inside. My mom wanted nothing to do with their kind of music, devil's music she called it, and certainly didn't want to give me the chance to meet the musical idols that she thought were undermining my morals. Against my protests, my mom had sent John Lennon and Brian Epstein packing, denying John the chance to talk to his idol – and denying me the chance to meet mine.

"Hi, George, I'm David," I said breathlessly. "I don't know if you even remember this, but one time you came to my house ..."

"That's right. And your mother wouldn't let you come out. At least that's what the lads told me when they got back to the car."

I could see that he was still amused by the incident, and for a moment I again felt like a little kid.

"Do you want to see Elvis?" I asked.

"When he's not busy."

"Come with me," I said, leading him to Elvis' dressing room. When we reached the dressing room door, I promised him I'd be right back.

"Hey, Elvis, George Harrison's here!" I said as I burst into the room. The rest of the entourage looked at me as if I'd lost my mind.

"It doesn't matter who's here, we're getting ready to do a show!" Joe snapped. Elvis saw the look in my eyes as the men in the room deflated my barely controlled enthusiasm.

"No, it's alright, guys," he interrupted. "I can say hi to George."

The men in the room shot daggers at me as I retrieved my new friend to greet Elvis. They exchanged quick greetings, and Elvis told Joe to make sure that George had the best seat in the house.

As it happened, that seat would be right next to me, on the speaker cabinet overlooking the stage.

Although I had gone to several concerts, I'd never seen a show from this vantage point. The energy of the sold-out crowd was swelling with each moment that passed. I was intoxicated by the emotion that filled the air; it was thick with love and adoration for the man I'd only known as my big brother. I felt as if all 22,000 of those screaming fans were fueling the swirling emotions inside of me. The lights dimmed and the screaming grew even louder. As the theme song from "2001" began to play, I saw Elvis, flanked by Sonny, Red, and Joe, walking toward the stage.

In many ways, it was like looking at him for the first time. It wasn't just the hair or the jumpsuit, there was something different that had overtaken him. Elvis had a charismatic presence that I already knew first-hand, but that charisma seemed to grow as he neared the stage. I could feel the hair standing up on my neck and knew that I would never see him the same way again. He looked like a god, and as he hit the stage, mass hysteria broke loose and screaming fans crushed toward the stage to worship him.

Fame

Although I had known him for most of my life, I suddenly felt hypnotized by Elvis' presence. It was absolutely unrivaled by any other event I had experienced in my life. I looked around and felt completely overwhelmed. The evening seemed beyond surreal. I was sitting on the side of the stage, watching what was the most powerful musical experience I had encountered in my life – and I was sharing it with George Harrison. I alternated between being starstruck by what I saw on stage and being numb with disbelief each time I looked over my shoulder and saw George Harrison sitting next to me, as completely enthralled with the concert as I was.

Colonel Parker would later explain to me that Elvis wasn't just a concert, he was an historical event. Unless someone had seen him perform, they couldn't really understand that line of thinking. But having been there, I knew that he was nothing less than a legendary figure who made an impact each and every time he took the stage, and would for generations to come.

The shows in Madison Square Garden were huge; four sold-out shows in three days. Each day was a whirlwind of new experiences, and by the time we left the Big Apple, I was already beginning to feel comfortable in my new world. There were women – not girls – waiting to meet anyone associated with Elvis, and if I had come to New York feeling like a boy I was certainly leaving it feeling like a man.

We flew into Fort Wayne, Indiana on June 12 and Elvis performed his sold-out concert before we all retired to the hotel. We would stay the night, then fly on to Evansville, Indiana, the next day for a show there. By the time we got back to the hotel, the crowds were eagerly awaiting our arrival. I was beginning to understand why Elvis needed a bodyguard. Although I had grown up with fans crowding around Graceland trying to get a glimpse of Elvis, I had never seen anything quite like the mass hysteria that I experienced on the road.

After Elvis and Lisa had retired to their room for the evening, the rest of us headed to the hotel bar where I had enough beers to send me to bed badly in need of some sleep. The rooms in Fort Wayne didn't hold a candle to what we had enjoyed in New York. I lay in my bed at the Fort Wayne Hilton, trying in vain to fall asleep. Outside my window, I could hear fans chanting for Elvis, demanding a glimpse of him.

"We want the King! We want the King!"

"Jesus!" I growled through gritted teeth, pulling the pillow over my head.

"We want the King!"

It sounded even louder. I tossed and turned for a few minutes, hoping the crowds would disappear. As their chanting continued, I threw back the covers and stormed out onto the balcony.

"Hey! Shut up down there!" I screamed.

The crowd grew hopefully quiet at my appearance, but quickly realized that I wasn't Elvis.

"Where's the King? We want the King!" shouted one woman.

"Yeah, right. Go home!" I shouted back.

"Who the hell are you?" yelled a male fan.

"I'm his brother, that's who. Who the hell are you?"

"You're an asshole! We want the King!" another fan screamed.

"Yeah? Well get in line and buy a damn ticket!"

I looked down at the largely female crowd and realized there were some women who might be worth getting into the show. I walked into my room, grabbed the key off my dresser and made my way back to the balcony.

"You wanna meet the King? You gotta go through me. Bring your sweet ass up here!"

With that, I tossed the key in the direction of the prettiest group of girls below.

"You're an idiot," someone shouted.

"And you're a bunch of peasants. Be gone!" I said, sweeping my hand above the crowd before throwing my beer can into their midst.

I walked back into my room, closing the door behind me and hoping their chanting would eventually fade. Damn fans, I thought as I crawled back into my bed. I pulled the covers over my head in hopes of drowning out the crowd, only to be disturbed by a sharp knock on the door. What the hell now?

Through the peephole in the hotel door, I could make out the face of a woman. One of the guys must have ordered room service, and she had the wrong room. I opened the door and saw a rather unattractive girl standing before me, a big smile on her face.

"What? I didn't order any ..."

As she happily dangled my room key in front of her, I remembered flinging it over the balcony moments earlier. She was bringing room service, but it was definitely not what I would have ordered.

"Okay, sweetie, hit the road," I said, grabbing my key from her hand. I might have been drunk, but I wasn't *that* drunk. I slammed the door behind her and tossed the key back on my dresser.

"Peasants," I said to myself with a giggle as I drunkenly collapsed back onto my bed. The noise of the crowd was finally subsiding, and I gratefully crawled under the covers and passed out.

The next day began in the usual way – with a trip to Elvis' room for breakfast. It was about two o'clock in the afternoon when I roused myself from bed and made my way to his suite. I opened the door and was surprised to see that most of the guys already were assembled there. Colonel Parker, Vernon, Sonny, Red and Joe all were sitting in the room, which fell silent as I pushed the door open.

"Hey! What's up, guys?" I asked, looking around the room to locate the breakfast spread.

"Have you seen this?" Elvis asked, holding up a newspaper.

"No," I said, completely oblivious. "Something happen in Vietnam?"

"No, THIS," Elvis replied, dropping the paper on the table in front of me. The headline running across the top of the page read, "Presley Brother Belligerent To Fans."

I could feel the blood in my veins turning to ice in an instant. I scanned the story, which gave an unfortunately accurate account of my interaction with fans from the balcony earlier that morning.

"We're not going to have any of this," Elvis said adamantly.

"But Elvis ..."

"Don't 'but' me," he returned vehemently.

Colonel Parker broke his customary silence to join in with a stern warning.

"He's right. We're not going to have this at all," he said. "If this happens again, you'll be on your way home. I'm not going to say it but once. This is not going to happen again."

"It's not!" Vernon added, and I saw that my stepfather's eyes were blazing with anger.

"You're goddamn right, it's not," Elvis added.

"Elvis ..." I began, stammering to defend myself.

"Who do you think pays the bills? The fans, that's who. They're not 'peasants,' David. They're the reason you're here, and I love them all."

I remained silent as he launched into a tirade that went on for a couple of minutes but seemed to last for hours. He ended it with the severe command, "Now get out of my sight."

I did as I was told, returning to my room still stinging from the verbal lashing I had received. I was hung over, hungry and humiliated. It was the first time Elvis had ever lost his temper with me, and I knew now that I never wanted to feel that wrath again. The experience had been devastating. Not only had Elvis yelled at me, he had done it in front of Vernon, Colonel Parker and the rest of the guys which was terribly embarrassing.

A few minutes later there was a knock on the door. I opened it to find Joe standing there. His demeanor was brusque and businesslike, far from the camaraderie usually shared amongst the rest of the guys.

"You're riding in another car tonight," he said, giving me the details of when I needed to be ready. I nodded, realizing the extent of my actions and wishing I could just erase everything I had said and done the night before.

Even my brother Ricky kept me at arms' length, and our ride from the hotel to the airport was a silent one. I took my place on the plane and might as well have been invisible; none of the guys spoke to me or even acknowledged that I was there. The last car arrived, carrying Elvis, Red, Sonny, Vernon and Lisa, and as they made their way onto the plane Elvis was all smiles – until he saw me. His gaze turned wooden and his eyes seemed to look right through me.

"Hey, Elvis..."

He continued walking right past me without speaking, and even Lisa didn't look my way. I sat in silence for the entire plane ride, watching the guys play cards and joke around with one another, all the while acting as if I weren't even there. Obviously I had broken a cardinal rule, thus earning the wrath of everyone.

We touched down around six o'clock and had just enough time to go through the ritual of preparing for the show. Everything about the routine was the same, but it felt entirely different. For the first time, I was on the outside looking in, and I suddenly felt very small, vulnerable and alone. I just wished the night would end and I could find myself in a different hotel, sleeping off this living nightmare that I had created for myself.

We didn't stay overnight in Evansville, but instead flew on to Chicago, the next stop on the tour. I climbed back aboard the plane, knowing I was in for a long and lonely flight. Elvis retired immediately to his bedroom and I sat there in my now familiar isolation, waiting for the miles to pass.

Ricky finally came out of Elvis' room and spoke to me for the first time that day.

"He wants to see you," Ricky said, gesturing to the back of the plane.

I didn't know what to expect as I opened his bedroom door, but I figured it was probably a good sign that he was even talking to me. Even another tongue-lashing would be better than the silent treatment.

"David, we can't have this," he said before I'd even closed the door behind me. "I expect mistakes, but it can't happen again. I love you, David, and it's all cool now, but it can't ever happen again."

"Yes sir," I said, heaving a sigh of relief.

"C'mere," he said with a grin, and gave me a big hug. I don't know that I had ever felt quite that relieved before in my life. I promised not to screw up like that again and made my way back to where the rest of the guys were already kicking back with some beers.

"I bet he kicked your ass good," Lamar said.

"No," I said. "Fortunately, I think he's done with that part."

"You learn your lesson?"

"Yes sir. I have learned my lesson."

It was true. I had learned a tremendous lesson about respect for the fans, for the people who kept the business running. But most of all, I had learned just how important it was to remain on Elvis' good side. Of course, it wasn't the last time I got into trouble, but it was the last time I got in that much trouble with Elvis. I made damn sure of that.

Street Fighting Man

We did a total of eight cities on my first tour with Elvis, performing about fifteen shows. By the time we returned to Memphis, the shows had blurred together in my mind, with the faces of screaming fans seeming to morph into one. I was exhilarated by the experience, making the month-long break we spent at Graceland feel as if it were dragging on forever. I was ready to get out from under my mother's roof and get back on the road, into a new life that I had wholeheartedly embraced. I no longer had the patience for slow, southern living.

I would pass the time at home by hanging out with my friends, riding motorcycles and such, and going to the movies with Elvis and the guys. While the rest of the world slept, we would spend all night at the movie theater watching pre-released films. This is something we did every night as long as I could remember.

I was hanging out with my friend Robert one night, and had just taken a lick of windowpane acid, when the phone rang. It was my brother Ricky saying that Elvis wanted everyone at the theater that night to see a new movie called "A Clockwork Orange."

I begged Ricky to get me out of the evening, knowing that the acid would soon be kicking in and the last place I wanted to be was next to Elvis and his shiny new narcotics badge. But Elvis was adamant about family, and he wanted us all to be together that night.

I sat as far away from him as I could, but since there were only about fifteen or twenty people in the theater, it was almost impossible to slip off his radar screen. Once the acid took hold, I started laughing and running my hand through the air, watching it turn colors.

Elvis watched me for a few moments, then asked Ricky what the hell was wrong with me.

"I dunno. I think he's been drinking tonight," Ricky said, doing his best to cover for me, but Elvis wasn't buying it. He walked over to me, putting his face directly in front of mine.

"What's wrong with you?"

"What? I ..." I looked at Elvis, who was eyeing me suspiciously. Somehow, the look on his face struck me as funny. I burst out laughing.

"What's so funny?"

"Nothing!" I protested. "I just think this movie is funny."

Elvis watched as I sat in my seat, shaking with uncontrollable laughter.

"You little son of a bitch, you've been taking acid, haven't you?"

"No sir!" I promised him, suddenly watching the world come back into focus. I was rebellious, and I'd give Elvis a hard time, but I still wanted him to respect me. Being on the road together had created a new bond, a new respect for each other. I didn't want anything to come between us, and I knew he hated street drugs. He would never allow me to be in his inner circle if he knew about my recreational drug use, so I faked it the best I could. That was good enough to fool Elvis, and that was all that mattered to me.

We celebrated our impending departure with a huge Fourth of July celebration at Graceland. I was relieved to see our time in Memphis coming to an end, as I was eager to see what lie in store for me in the next few weeks. We were headed to Los Angeles for about a month, where Elvis would rehearse for his upcoming Las Vegas engagement.

Unlike all of the other times I had traveled with Elvis, I learned that we were flying out on a commercial airplane. I had no idea how that was going to work - how do you escort Elvis Presley through an airline terminal and onto an airplane without absolute mayhem ensuing? He drew crowds everywhere he went, so I couldn't imagine that it would be any different at the airport.

The limousines arrived to pick us up while we said our goodbyes to family. Elvis was eager to get to L.A.; Priscilla and Lisa Marie had already moved into a house there and he missed his little girl. Although Elvis saw his daughter regularly, it would be even easier for him to visit her in the same city. We drove to the airport, but instead of going to the terminal, the limousines veered off the traditional route, driving right onto the tarmac. An American Airlines plane was waiting for us, and I could see the heads of passengers inside. Our limousine pulled up alongside the plane. As we got out of the cars, I glanced up and saw that all eyes from inside the airplane were upon us. People were pointing and women were struggling to get a better view. I smiled to myself as I watched the scene.

We walked up the steps right into the first class section, which had been closed off from the rest of the passengers. When the plane landed, we were already in our limousines and driving away before the rest of the passengers were allowed to deplane. I had to admit, if I had to fly on a commercial plane, flying with Elvis was definitely the way to go.

In Los Angeles, we settled into the house that Elvis owned. It was smaller than what we were accustomed to at Graceland, but the amenities – the California weather, a gorgeous pool, all the freedom a teenage boy could want – more than made up for the smaller space. We had only been there a day when Elvis made good on his promise to start my martial arts training.

He took me and my older brother Billy, who had just started working for him, to meet Ed Parker at his Kenpo Karate School in Santa Monica. Ed, a ninth-degree black belt, was one of the most respected martial arts masters in the world. Ed was teaching a class when we arrived, and a man named Tom Kelly greeted us warmly.

Elvis explained to Tom why we were there, and when Ed came over to say hello, Elvis didn't introduce me, but merely asked Ed to do a demonstration for us. Ed was more than happy to oblige.

We sat down along the wall, while Ed's students lined up against the wall on the other side of the room. Ed stood in the center of the room and called three of his higher ranked belts, including Tom Kelly, to join him on the floor. The three men positioned themselves around Ed, who waited for a moment, then nodded his head.

All three men attacked him with a flurry of blows and kicks that were useless against Ed's catlike reflexes. My jaw dropped as I watched him stealthily avoid the graceful, but potentially deadly moves of his opponents. At that moment, I knew that I wanted to learn everything I could from this man. Hell, I wanted to *be* this man.

The demonstration went on for about an hour. The skilled movements I saw mesmerized me. Although I had seen Elvis practice karate, it was different watching the students in the school as Ed Parker led them. The room had the same kind of energy I'd felt backstage at concerts with Elvis, and I had become addicted to that rush. I knew that I would do whatever it took to become proficient in karate.

We went into Ed's room after the demonstration.

"So, this is the guy you've been telling me about," Ed said, a slight smile playing at his lips.

"Yep. This is David," Elvis said, patting my shoulder in a fatherly manner.

Ed looked me over and shook his head.

"They grow 'em big down south, don't they?"

"Yeah, yeah they do, Ed. I want you to personally undertake his training."

Ed looked at me and nodded. I felt completely exhilarated. Ed was much like Elvis in many ways; he had the same kind of magnetism that drew people in. I wanted to please him as much as I wanted to please Elvis; I was ready to do whatever he asked of me.

I started taking karate every day, going to classes twice a day whenever I could. We didn't exactly have a rigorous schedule; much of our day was spent poolside, soaking up the sun, and at night we would head to RCA studios for Elvis' rehearsals. That left plenty of time to work on martial arts.

We were in Los Angeles to get ready for a month-long engagement at the Las Vegas Hilton. Fans took advantage of the intimate setting in Vegas and would rush the stage, trying to get as close to the King as they could.

It was the first time I got to use the skills I was being trained in; my nights were spent on the periphery of Elvis' stage area, catching over-eager women as they made their break for the stage. It wasn't exactly dangerous work, but it was certainly a lot more strenuous than our previous gigs.

Elvis did two shows a night for thirty days, and we all were beginning to feel the strain of the non-stop schedule. We recuperated by sleeping late, then catching a Kenpo workout before sunning by the pool. By early evening, it was time to get ready for that night's shows and do it all over again.

I returned from the pool one afternoon to find the phone in my room ringing. When I picked it up, I heard Lamar Fike's frantic voice on the other end of the line.

"David, it's Lamar. Get down here. Now!"

"What's wrong?!"

"We've got a problem. Just get your ass down here!"

He slammed the phone down and I scrambled to find a pair of jeans and T-shirt to pull on as I threw my wet swimming trunks on the floor. I had no idea what to expect. I couldn't think of anything that I had done recently that would have me in such big trouble, and the tone in Lamar's voice told me there was something rather significant going on.

I ran down the hallway, pushing my way past the security guards that kept fans away from Elvis' suite. Pushing the door open, the first thing I saw was the look of horror on the faces of Red and

Sonny. Everyone else was looking at Elvis, who was standing in the center of the room, waving an M-16.

"You chicken-shit sons of bitches!" he screamed, edging closer toward the two terrified bodyguards. "You're either with me or against me. If you won't kill him, I'll find someone who will!"

"Boss, hey, just settle down, man," Red pleaded. "Come on, be cool..."

"Yeah, Boss, easy," Sonny chimed in, moving closer with the cautiousness of someone approaching a wounded animal.

Elvis moved forward to meet Sonny, putting the barrel of the M-16 squarely in Sonny's face.

"You piece of shit! I oughta blow your fuckin' head off right now!"

The blood drained from Sonny's face and I found myself frozen in place, not sure what I had wandered into or what I was supposed to do about it. Across the room, I could see Vernon was in a similar state of mind, not sure what to do, but sure that he needed to do something.

"Son, hey, son," he said, moving toward Elvis and putting his hand gingerly on his son's shoulder.

"Come on, now, son. You don't want to do this. Everything's going to be okay ... please, just let it go. Put the gun down."

Elvis waited for a moment, breathing hard and uncertain what to do. He didn't want to back down, but he knew that Vernon was right.

"You bunch of damn cowards!" he yelled, slamming the M-16 to the floor. As the M-16 hit the floor, it only added to the tension of the moment. The room was still, with everyone white-faced and terrified of what had transpired.

Elvis turned and stormed past me toward his bedroom.

"Get the doc up here," he spat in my face as he pushed me aside. I couldn't dial the phone fast enough.

Dr. Nick was there in moments, and the rest of the guys were resuming their activity, moving cautiously but still going about the tasks at hand. I followed Dr. Nick into the bedroom, trying to explain what I'd seen, but Dr. Nick didn't need to hear it. He looked knowingly at Elvis lying on the bed, reached into his bag and pulled out a handful of pills.

"Here, take these. They'll help you rest," he promised.

Right now I felt like I could use a rest. As I watched, Elvis put the entire handful of pills in his mouth, then washed them down with a glass of water. He collapsed back onto his bed, waiting for the pills to take effect. The doc put a bottle of pills on the nightstand, joining an already ample display.

"Call me if you need me," he told Elvis, then stood and walked past me without saying anything further.

I stood in the silence of the darkened room, watching Elvis as he stared blankly at the wall. This wasn't the man I knew, and for all the strange things I had already seen on the road, I hadn't seen this one coming. This behavior was completely out of character, at least based on my experience with him over the last 12 years.

"Are you – are you alright, man?" I asked him tentatively. He didn't look at me, and just kept staring at the wall.

"Nothin' the doc can't fix. Now – get outta here and leave me alone," he said.

He wasn't angry anymore; his voice sounded flat and lifeless. I did as I was told, slipping out of the room and leaving the suite silently. I didn't know what had just happened.

Things are different on the road, David. I could hear Lamar's words echoing through my head. *No kidding*, I thought. As much as I'd come to like life on the road, I wasn't so sure I liked this new version of Elvis.

Returning to my room, I stood outside and stared at the Las Vegas skyline, trying to make sense of what I had just witnessed. I heard someone enter my hotel room, and in moments Lamar was standing beside me, saying nothing.

"You gotta smoke, Lamar?"

"You don't smoke!"

"I do now," I said. Lamar complied, pulling out a pack of smokes and lighting mine before igniting one for himself. He took a long pull on his cigarette before speaking.

"You had no idea what you were gettin' yourself into, didja David?"

"I didn't sign up for this," I said, taking a drag off my cigarette and immediately going into a coughing spasm. Lamar was right – I didn't smoke.

"Are ya sure ya still wanna do this?"

"I don't get it, Lamar! What's wrong with him?!"

"Hey, it's been a tough year. The tours, the road, the pressure. The ex leavin' him for a karate instructor, then rubbin' his face in it by goin' public. He's humiliated. That's all."

"But – but he was gonna *shoot* those guys!"

53

Lamar smiled.

"Nah. He wasn't gonna shoot nobody. That was just his ego talkin'. It's as wide as a Cadillac grill. That was just his way of blowin' off steam."

"Well, he sure scared the hell out of me," I said, taking another attempt at inhaling my cigarette smoke and getting the same reaction. Lamar said nothing as I finished coughing.

"And the drugs!" I continued. "In high school, Mr. Nixon's personal federal narcotics agent in there wanted ME to be a narc. ME! And now he's poppin' a pill for everything!"

"I know, I know," Lamar agreed. "Too much medication and too many doctors."

"Then get rid of the damned doctors, Lamar!"

Lamar shook his head.

"Won't happen. He's very sensitive about his medication."

"That's bullshit. That's not medication – he's doin' drugs! He's not sick. He catches me blowin' a doob and he won't talk to me for a week. Like I shot the Pope or somethin'!"

"Look, David, the doc prescribes it, and that makes it legal. Around here, that makes all the difference."

I stood there for a moment, contemplating my dilemma and feeling my frustration collide with my confusion. Maybe I just didn't belong here. Maybe I was better off when I didn't know the real Elvis, when everything was all about Graceland, good times, and family.

"Hey, Lamar, you know what you said ... about wantin' to do this?"

"Yeah?"

"Man, I just don't know anymore..."

He turned to me, taking on a fatherly stance. I could see the sympathy in his eyes and felt like he truly wanted me to understand the scope of my decision.

"Listen, David, I've been around a long, long time, seen it all, and there's one thing ya gotta understand. There's no delegation of authority around here. Nobody gets a vote – it's a one-man show."

"Yeah? Then why the hell does he need us? Why are we even here?"

"To keep up the image, that's why. And to protect him from everything out there," he responded, nodding toward the skyline. "That's part of your job now – to protect him from everyone and everything out there."

"Who the hell is gonna protect him from himself?"

Lamar stood quiet for a few moments, contemplating my words, but not answering them. He stubbed his cigarette out on my balcony rail.

"I better go check on him. You comin'?"

"In a minute."

He walked out and I fixed my gaze over the skyline. It was another beautiful night and from my balcony, it seemed as if I had the world at my fingertips. From the outside, I was part of rock 'n' roll royalty. Inside, I felt like a court jester, performing for the King and his court and doing his bidding. This wasn't what I had expected when I stepped on that first plane to New York.

After thirteen years with Elvis, I thought I knew him. But life on the road was showing me a side of him that I didn't know existed, and in that moment I wished that I had never seen it. I remembered what he had said a few weeks earlier at the press conference in New York, "The image is one thing, the person's another."

That was turning out to be truer than I had imagined, and I was no longer sure which Elvis was the person, and which one was the image.

School's Out Forever

As the calendar would have it, I would soon have the chance to test my desire to leave the road and clear my head. For most kids my age, August meant back-to-school, and it wasn't a surprise when Vernon announced that my mom had called and wanted me to be home for the start of the school year. I didn't want to go back to school, but in many ways I was ready for a break from the road.

My sophomore year of high school meant that I would have to enroll in its ROTC program. Everything about me was anti-military; I was anti-political, anti-war, anti-authority and definitely anti-ROTC. I knew the ROTC program involved uniforms, and when it came time to get a military haircut, I knew that I couldn't do it. I walked out, leaving school for good. At home, I lied to my mom, telling her that someone had put acid in my food.

"School's not like it used to be, Mom," I convinced her. "It's not safe anymore."

Horrified by the story I told her, she agreed that I didn't need to be there, and made no arguments when I picked up the phone to call Elvis.

"School's not working out for me," was all I told him.

"I didn't think it would," Elvis replied. "Come on back to Vegas."

I eagerly jumped on the next available plane. My final year of high school had lasted exactly three days.

The Las Vegas gig was winding down by the time I joined them. Before leaving, Elvis held a press conference, announcing a concert in Hawaii that would be broadcast via satellite around the world. It would be an epic event, and a live album was being released from the concert as well.

We spent a couple of weeks in Memphis before heading back to the West Coast for the rest of the fall. It was good to be back in L.A. I resumed my Kenpo training with Ed Parker, enjoying the art more each day. I may still have been a loose cannon on my own time, but Kenpo was teaching me how to focus. It gave me mental clarity that I would eventually learn to utilize outside the ring as well.

Elvis did a couple of small tours in October and November, and his single, "Burning Love," was burning up the charts. It was a good time to be a part of his world, as we all knew that the television special from Hawaii would only boost his popularity.

We ended our West Coast tour with a show in Hawaii, at the same place we would be doing the live concert in just two months. We stayed in Hawaii for Thanksgiving, and it was there that I had my first real run-in with one of Elvis' bodyguards. By now, I had learned that my position as Elvis' stepbrother carried plenty of weight, and I no longer felt like the seventeen-year-old kid that I was. Most of the time, I didn't feel the need to listen to the adults around me, preferring instead to forge my own way in the world.

I was hanging out on the balcony one afternoon with Sonny, hanging over the railing and watching the bikini-clad world below me.

"Don't lean over the rail like that, you're gonna fall," cautioned Sonny.

"I'm not gonna fall," I shot back, aggravated by his fatherly demeanor.

"I mean it, David, don't lean over the rail."

"Shut up!" I said, glowering back at him.

Sonny had had enough of my cocky attitude and now he put his face in mine. "How'd you like me to kick your little ass?" he demanded, clearly perturbed.

I stood up, using every inch of my six-foot-three-inch frame to my advantage. I looked at him square in the eyes.

"I don't think that's a very good idea," I said as menacingly as I could muster.

"You know, David, you can't just run around being a little smart-ass like that all the time."

"What're you gonna do about it?" I taunted.

"I oughtta kick your ass right here," he said, holding back from hauling off from doing just that.

"You'll have to take that up with Elvis," I snarled back. Sonny glared at me for a moment before tossing his cigarette over the balcony and stomping off. I laughed to myself and continued watching the sunbathing beauties below my balcony. I was untouchable, I thought, and Sonny knew it.

The phone in my room rang within minutes and I hastily agreed to Elvis' command to meet him in his suite. He was waiting for me when I got there, and the look on his face told me he wasn't too pleased about something. Elvis wasted no time in getting to the point.

"You got a problem with Sonny?" he asked.

"Well, I was just leanin' on a rail and he got all smart-mouth and bossy with me," I explained. Elvis gave me a long look and shook his head.

"Listen. He probably just didn't want you to fall. You need to listen to these guys, David. If you keep disrespecting them, you're gonna pay for it."

I knew better than to argue back.

"You don't want to mess with Sonny," he continued. "You need to watch what you say."

I nodded, knowing that it was pointless to try and defend my actions at that point. But I also knew it probably wasn't the last time we'd be having this conversation.

Christmas was spent at Graceland, and when we returned to Los Angeles Elvis began rehearsing in earnest for the live broadcast from Hawaii. I threw myself back into karate training and quickly earned my yellow belt.

I had worked so hard for that first belt, and was about to burst with excitement by the time I got back to the house. Priscilla was at the house when I got there, so she was among the first to hear my good news.

"Look what I got!" I said as I came into the house, as excited as a little kid at Christmas.

Some of the guys were hanging around playing cards, and they looked up briefly, but were not really interested in my newfound passion. Priscilla came over to me and gave me a big hug.

"You know, David, I am so proud of you," she told me. "Of all the people I've ever met, you are one of the few people who can do whatever they decide to do. Remember that."

I nodded. Priscilla had always had my love and admiration; she was like a big sister to me and I thought the world of her.

"Have you done any tournaments yet?" she asked me, and I shook my head.

"Not yet, but I wanna."

"Well, there's a tournament coming up this weekend. Why don't you come to it and try competing?"

I didn't know if I was ready for a tournament, but I was certainly ready to find out. I told her I would think about it and give her a call.

"Where's Elvis?" I asked, eager to show him my belt.

"He's outside by the pool," she said. "I've got to go – give me a call about that tournament."

I promised I would, then raced outside to show Elvis what I had accomplished that day.

He looked like a bronzed god, lying by the pool with his shirt open and the sun illuminating his handsome face. His girlfriend, Lisa, was by his side, enjoying the California weather. I broke the silence of their world as I ran out of the house, yelling for Elvis at the top of my lungs. I was still wearing my karate uniform as I approached them. When Elvis opened his eyes, I proudly pointed to my belt.

"Look what I got!"

Elvis smiled and gave a small nod.

"That's pretty impressive," he said, rising to his feet and assuming a traditional defensive karate position. "Show me what you learned."

I took my fighting stance and made a couple of quick moves, striking him as hard as I could in the midsection. He was completely caught off guard and reeled backwards, the shock in his eyes quickly turning to anger. He hadn't expected me to actually make contact with him, only to show him my form. Elvis took a moment to compose himself while I waited to see if I was in trouble.

Finally, he exhaled heavily and resumed a fighting stance.

"Let me see you do that again," he ordered.

I took my stance, feeling like the badass I knew I was, and went after him again. This time around, he blocked my punch and caught me with a fist to the face. It dropped me in my tracks.

Elvis had studied martial arts long enough to know how to hit me without breaking anything I might want to use later – such as my nose – but his blow left me dizzy and stunned on the pavement. Elvis was standing over me, ready to help me stand back up. I lay there for a second and, as the reality of what had just happened set in, I jumped to my feet.

"What the f..." I began, my temper raging.

"Hold on there, young man," Elvis said, immediately jumping back into his fighting stance. "You don't even want to think about it."

I looked at him, ready to take him down.

"Don't ever forget this, David," Elvis said, looking firmly at me. "I may have taught you everything you know, but I haven't taught you everything *I* know."

I glared at him, knowing he was right but frustrated by the truth of the situation. The anger slowly began to dissipate and Elvis and I both relaxed, ending with a hug as he told me how proud he was of me for earning my first belt. His point was made, and well taken: As much of a badass as I was, I was no match for him. He wanted to make sure that no matter how many belts I accumulated, I never forgot that.

Later that day, Ed and some of his students came to the house to work out with Elvis. I was going through some techniques with Elvis when they arrived, and they watched for a few minutes as we finished up. Elvis motioned for one of the third degree black belts to come over.

"David, show him that move you showed me today."

"Well, last time I showed you, it hurt," I said, looking pointedly at Elvis. Elvis' face showed an instant flash of anger and he held up one finger as a fatherly warning. He wasn't about to be shown up by some punk kid with a yellow belt in a room full of black belts.

Feeling cocky, I took my fighting stance and the black belt came toward me. He knew he was only facing a yellow belt, so he wasn't expecting much in the way of maneuvers. Elvis stood back and watched as I threw a punch that dropped my opponent to his knees. For the second time that afternoon, I saw the stunned face of a higher belt looking up at me.

He jumped to his feet and came after me.

"I'll kick your ass, you little son-of-a-bitch," he said as he got in position.

"Come on," I taunted, resuming my stance. "Bring it!"

Ed Parker had watched our exchange and now he stepped in between us.

"Don't do that," he cautioned me.

"But – Elvis told me to..."

"But I'm telling you not to," Ed returned, his voice even but emphatic.

"He ain't so bad," I said, tossing my head cockily toward the black belt. Ed shook his head.

"You don't want to find out how bad he is," he said.

Elvis walked over, obviously amused.

"Ed, I already told him. I taught him everything he knows, but I can't teach him everything we know."

The men laughed, enjoying the moment, and I suddenly found myself embarrassed by my own actions. It was a lesson I needed to learn, but one that would take years to sink in. It would be decades before I learned to channel the anger inside of me, harness my energy, and use it to my advantage. Karate was one thing that helped me learn to do that, and Elvis was another. Karate became the unbreakable bond that we shared, and he taught me lessons that transcended the mat.

Everybody Was Kung Fu Fighting

I decided to take Priscilla up on her invitation to participate in a tournament. It was Elvis' fanaticism with karate that led him entourage Priscilla to train in martial arts, and she began working with an instructor named Mike Stone. Mike Stone was a handsome man and the two soon had more than a student-teacher relationship.

Although Elvis hadn't been faithful, he was devastated when Priscilla moved out of Graceland in early 1972, taking Lisa Marie with her to Los Angeles. I tried not to get too involved in the details, as it wasn't my business and, at seventeen years old, it just wasn't something I cared to hear about. I had always adored Priscilla, and I was sorry to see her go. All I really knew about the situation was that she had met someone else. It wasn't talked about at home, and it sure wasn't brought up with Elvis, so the details had never been shared with me.

Since she had remained friends with Elvis, it wasn't much of a surprise when she would show up at our Los Angeles house. I was pleased that she thought enough of me to invite me to participate in a karate tournament. Of course, I was also eager to see how I fared in competition.

My friend Nancy and few other friends of hers went to the tournament together. I found Priscilla, who was standing with Mike

Stone. She introduced him as her friend, and then we went our separate ways to compete in the day's activities.

At the end of the day, both Mike and I had won our divisions, and Priscilla recommended that we all go to her house in Marina Del Ray to celebrate.

I knew how Elvis felt about Mike, making me feel awkward about going to her house, but I didn't want to hurt my friendship with Priscilla either. I couldn't say that I had anything against Mike, but I knew how Elvis would feel about it, and that made me uncomfortable. I wanted to be around Priscilla, but I was also afraid of being discovered and having Elvis question my loyalty.

At their house, I was uncertain of what to say to Mike. I wanted to keep my relationship with Priscilla, so I didn't want to hurt her feelings by declining her invitation, though I felt more than a bit awkward about the evening.

Mike was a nice guy, but I just didn't know what to think of him. Priscilla pulled me aside, explaining to me who Mike really was, and how their relationship had begun, and then blossomed. It was more information than I wanted, and only served to make me even more uncomfortable. I assured her that I was okay with it, wanting her to know that I didn't blame her, but in my mind that didn't change the fact I felt pulled between her and Elvis. Talking with Mike felt like I was consorting with the enemy; befriending the guy who was responsible for the breakup of the marriage of the guy I was sworn to protect.

At that point in my life, it wasn't something I was ready to handle, and as much as I adored Priscilla, I truly wanted to keep her and Mike at a distance. It was just much less complicated that way.

I became as obsessed with Kenpo Karate as Elvis was, and could not get enough the martial arts. I trained hard; as soon as I recovered from one workout I was ready for the next. The second time I participated in a tournament, Elvis and Ed Parker accompanied me. I was entered in the Blue Belt Heavyweight Division and felt confident that I could take my division. When it was my turn to compete, I took my place on the mat and assumed my fighting stance.

My opponent made the first move, kicking me squarely in the nose – something that was specifically against the rules of the tournament. Automatically, my hand flew to my face and when I pulled it back, I saw my own blood covering my hand. That was all it took to set me off. He had repositioned himself and as he moved in to deliver a punch, I flew into action, landing a powerful ridge hand blow to my opponent's shoulder.

It sounded like a gun being fired as I made contact with his shoulder. He dropped to the floor in pain, and we would all soon discover that I had dislocated his shoulder. But in the moment, the only thing I knew was that I was mad as hell about his dirty trick.

"Get up, you sorry son of a bitch," I screamed as I towered over him on the floor. "Come on, you piece of shit, I'm gonna kick your ass!"

We were no longer alone in the ring; referees had jumped in to keep me from following through on that threat, and Elvis and Ed weren't far behind them. Ed Parker grabbed the sleeve of my uniform.

"Get out of here, David. Just get out!" he said angrily, pointing toward the door. Both he and Elvis were fuming. Elvis grabbed me by the other arm and began propelling me toward the side of the ring.

"Come on, we're leaving," he said. I followed him to the door, my nose still bleeding, with Ed hot on my heels. Outside, we climbed into the waiting six-door Mercedes Benz and Elvis motioned for our driver to pull away.

Nobody said a word as we left. I kept waiting for someone to break the silence, knowing that it couldn't be me. Even getting chewed out would be better than being frozen out, I thought. We stared out the windows as our limousine drove down Santa Monica Boulevard, and when we pulled up to a stoplight, Elvis finally broke his silence.

"You know what, David? You need some discipline."

"Elvis, the guy hit me in the nose! I'm bleeding!"

"David, you hurt that guy bad! You dislocated his shoulder!"

"I don't give a shit. He kicked me in the nose!"

"Well, lemme tell you something, David. You need some control. You dropped this guy to the floor, and you tried doing the same damn thing to me. You can't do that, David. You would have killed that guy if we hadn't stepped in."

While we talked, a car full of girls had pulled up beside us. Recognizing the limousine, they were holding pieces of paper outside the window, waving them for Elvis to autograph. Elvis opened the door and took some of the papers, smiling as he began signing them. Although the light turned green, neither car moved as Elvis obliged his excited fans.

The car behind our limousine took exception to the extended wait. As the light remained green – and we remained stopped – the driver began to honk his horn. Elvis smiled and held up his hand, gesturing for them to give him just one more minute. The young men in the car responded with a few gestures of their own and began adding some rather unkind expletives to the honking of their horn.

From my place inside the limo, I leaned forward to see what all the commotion was about and knew from the looks of the guys behind us that I didn't want a piece of this fight. They were some rough-looking characters, and even if they hadn't outnumbered us, I got the feeling that a bloody nose would be the least of my problems with this group.

The light turned red and Elvis finished signing his autographs, and as he closed the door, the boys in the car behind us grew even bolder, yelling louder and laying on the horn. Just as the light turned green, Elvis had had enough, and stepped out of the car.

"Oh, shit," I muttered, knowing I had to do the same. I jumped out of my side and as the car of girls pulled away, the car behind us swerved into their spot and peeled out. Elvis tried unsuccessfully to hit the car as it went past him. He swore at them as they screeched past him, flipping him off and shouting obscenities.

"Get back in the car!" Elvis shouted at me. Then he screamed at the driver, "Catch those sons of bitches! Follow them!"

Our driver did as he was told, and Elvis opened the limousine's moon roof, standing up and watching the car as we pursued it. He had pulled out his .22 caliber pistol, and as we neared the car, he began shooting at its tires. It didn't take more than three or four shots before he hit a tire, sending the car careening to the side of the road.

Elvis dropped back inside the limo, smoothing his hair back.

"That'll teach those sons of bitches," he said. "Now – what were we discussing?"

69

Ed looked at him incredulously.

"I think we were discussing David needing discipline, Elvis," Ed answered, still taken aback by the scene he had just witnessed.

The speech Elvis had been delivering on self-control seemed to have lost its power for the moment. He was still mad at me, but he didn't have nearly as much room to talk as he'd had when the conversation began. Talk about the pot calling the kettle black. And people wondered why I never listened.

The next day I bought a peel-off sticker of the Kenpo Karate crest and went into Elvis' office to show it to him and offer it up as a sort of peace offering. He wasn't there, so I sat down and noticed his black, high-gloss Gibson guitar sitting in the corner. The crest was black with a white background, and I knew it would look stunning on the guitar, so I carefully placed it on the Gibson. I smiled to myself, knowing that Elvis would probably be upset when he first saw it, thinking I had defaced his prized guitar.

I admired my handiwork for a few moments, then decided to reposition the sticker. I pulled at the edge and realized that this was a permanent sticker, not a peel-off reusable sticker. At that moment, I knew I was dead as a doornail.

I tried again, knowing I had to be careful not to scratch the guitar's surface. Panic was rising inside of me as I realized what I had done.

"What are you doing?" I heard Elvis' voice behind me as he came down the stairs. I was in deep shit. He was going to kill me. I was sure of it.

"Um, nothing, I'm not doing anything, man."

I sat the guitar down, standing it against the wall with its face hidden. Elvis had a trace of a smile on his lips, knowing he had caught me in the middle of something, but still not sure what the nature of my activity was.

"What are you doing?" he asked again, this time with a laugh.

I knew I was busted. I might as well confess and take my medicine straight up, rather than trying to drag this out.

"Well, I sort of ... you know..."

I turned the guitar around so Elvis could see the sticker.

"David!" he exclaimed, grabbing the guitar from my hands. But his excitement wasn't born of anger, as I had expected.

"That's great! Where did you get that?"

Elvis was completely thrilled with the sticker, and it remained on his guitar. He even talked about it onstage, using it as an excuse to tell the adoring crowds about his passion for Kenpo Karate. As for me, I was just relieved. I knew that story could easily have gone in the opposite direction.

The King of The World

Iflew to Hawaii with Sonny and Joe the day before Elvis arrived for his televised "Aloha from Hawaii" concert. Each of us had different jobs to do; mine was to assist Joe in making sure that everything was in order just as Elvis had requested. There was definite electricity in the air with this show. Elvis was about to make history again; this was the first time such a concert would be broadcast around the world. It was going to be seen live in Australia, Japan, South Korea, Thailand, the Philippines and South Vietnam, with another thirty countries airing the live concert on a delayed tape.

When Elvis arrived at the airport the next day, camera crews followed him as he was transported to the hotel via helicopter. Surrounded by fans, we steered him toward a waiting Jeep, where Colonel Parker, Sonny, Red and I climbed in, along with Vernon, Joe and James Colley, and headed toward the hotel. Throngs of screaming fans had become commonplace, but there was something different this time around. I don't know if it was the camera crews or the energy that Elvis himself was feeling about the televised concert, but everything in the air felt electrifying.

At the hotel, we had some time to relax and enjoy our surroundings before the concerts. We had a pre-broadcast rehearsal concert on January twelfth, with the actual live televised show on January fourteenth. Elvis had commissioned a special jumpsuit for the occasion, and I could tell that he was more excited than usual about this performance. In fact, everyone seemed more excited than usual. We all knew this was big, but then, everything Elvis did was big. What remained to be seen was just how big Elvis could in fact make this concert.

The rehearsal went smoothly enough; Elvis was uncharacteristically nervous on the first song, but rebounded quickly and went on to perform a phenomenal concert. It set the stage for the live televised show two days later.

All of us could feel the the charge in the air as the performance time grew closer. The venue was completely sold out as always, and everyone seemed amped up for the performance.

Backstage before the concert, we could feel the anticipation of the waiting crowd. Elvis always seemed like a caged animal before his performances, pacing the floor, eager to get out on stage. This time, the fact that he'd be performing before the whole world only exacerbated that nervous energy.

I got the signal that he had ten minutes until show time, and I popped my head into his dressing room. Vernon, Lamar, a makeup artist and a hairstylist were the only other people in the room.

"Ten minutes, Boss," I told him.

Elvis nodded. I walked into the room, feeling the excitement that was emanating from him.

"Can I have a couple minutes?" he asked politely, and we all began moving toward the door.

"Not you, David," he said. "I need you to do something for me."

The door closed behind me, leaving us alone in the dressing room.

"Sure, Boss – what d'ya need?"

Elvis produced a small black bag from beneath his dressing room table.

"I need you to give me a shot," he said, pulling out a syringe and a small clear bottle of liquid. "I need ten cc's."

I looked at the syringe and bottle in the King's outstretched hand and stood there paralyzed, unable to move.

"Come on, David. Ten cc's," he repeated.

It was a command I hadn't expected and one I didn't know how to follow. I looked at him blankly.

"I- I'm not a doctor," I stammered.

"It's just B-12, David," he said, growing impatient. "Now give me the damn shot."

"Elvis, I don't know what this is. I can't do this."

"One day, you're gonna learn to do what I tell you," he said, clearly annoyed with me. "Either give me the shot or go get Dr. Nick. Now!"

I opened the door to the dressing room just as James Colley was about to enter. Elvis heaved a sigh of relief.

"James, get over here and gimme this shot," he said. "David, get the hell outta here."

That was an order I was willing to follow, and as James closed the door behind me, I went to my place on the side of the stage. By the time he joined us a few minutes later, I could see the tension in his body. He walked in circles, pacing in our small backstage area as the theme to "2001" began to play. I could hear the fans begin to scream.

"Elvis, are you okay?" I asked.

He looked at me with amusement.

"David, it was just B-12," he said before hitting the stage.

I watched as the King tended to his loyal kingdom. It was a powerful performance, one that was seen by more American households than Neil Armstrong's first walk on the moon. It was one of the all-time highs in his career, and as I watched him perform a flawless show, the only thing I could think was, "B-12, my ass!" I may have been a hot-headed, immature teenager, but I knew when I was being lied to.

After the Hawaii show, we headed back to Las Vegas, where Elvis was going to spend the month performing at the Hilton. Somewhere along the way, my excitement had faded, and I felt tired and burned out. My head was spinning from the contradictions that I found within my often surreal existence. The people that I had grown up with, people I thought I had known, were not at all what I had thought. And Elvis was the heartbreaker of them all. We had two realities: The people we were on the road, and the people we were at home. My young mind had trouble assimilating everything I had seen and experienced, and I desperately needed a break to regroup.

Elvis wasn't pleased with my decision to leave. He initially tried to talk me out of it, but knowing how stubborn I was, he eventually backed down. I could tell that he thought it was temporary, that I'd soon be calling him up and asking him to take me back on the road.

This wasn't like last time I left the tour, though. I wasn't leaving because my mom wanted me back home; this time, I was going home of my own free will. I wasn't sure what I would do, but I was fairly certain I could figure it out on my own.

Knowing that going back to school was out of the question for me, I returned to Memphis and immediately found a job working for Onyx Studios. Elvis had a friend by the name of Bill Browder who worked there, so it wasn't hard to get my foot in the door. I loved music and I knew I wanted to make a career out of it, but I still didn't feel like I had found the place in this business where I could fit in. I loved mixing music, loved sound engineering and the process that went into making the music come together. I even joined a band, playing drums on the weekends just for kicks.

At Onyx Studios, I worked hard and learned fast, eager to master the music business. I would tell Vernon about what I'd learned, and confided in him that I wanted to move to Nashville and get a job there.

Next thing I knew, I was offered a job in Nashville as assistant manager of RCA Records' music publishing division. It was a dream job, and I knew that the Presley name was the clout behind the phone call, but I didn't care. That was part of the privilege I had grown up with, and if it was going to help me land my dream job, I had no problem accepting it. I wasn't going to cut off my nose to spite my face.

I drove to Nashville in my 1972 Mach I Mustang, ready to begin my brand-new adult life. I was just 17 years old. One of my best friends, Larry Inman, had moved there a year earlier with his parents, so I stayed with them for about a month while I started my job and looked for a place to live. I loved being around Larry, but we now lived in completely different worlds. Although we were the same age, while he was enjoying his time in high school, I had been on the road with the King of Rock 'n' Roll. Our experiences were vastly different, but our friendship had thus far bridged whatever changes each of us had undergone.

Regardless of the fact that I was living in an adult world, I was still a boy at heart. After work, I hung out with Larry and his buddies, who had been out of school for a couple of hours before my workday was finished. The apartment Mom and Vernon helped me get soon became the place to hang out at on the weekends or after school. I'd go to their high school football games with them, watching the cheerleaders and sneaking beers during halftime.

I enjoyed Larry and his buddies, but I already knew that something was missing. I could feel the lure of the rock 'n' roll lifestyle calling me, begging me to come back and partake of its many available pleasures. Deep inside, I knew I wanted to try and make a "normal" life work, so I kept ignoring that call, trying to shove the genie back in the bottle, but the cork just never seemed to fit tight enough no matter how hard I tried to shove it back in.

My long hair, "TCB" necklace and "Elvis on tour" jacket inevitably accomplished at least two things: It impressed the girls while alienating their parents. Larry and his buddies knew all the cheerleaders at Franklin High School, and soon I was either friends with them, dating them, or both. Their parents were typically less than thrilled to see me showing up at their door, but I didn't really care. I wasn't there for them.

They were all beautiful girls, but I guess my serial dating was inevitable, given the experiences I'd had on the road. My own peers now seemed like kids to me, and although I desperately wanted to fit into their world, I knew that I didn't. The life experiences that I'd known were so far removed from theirs that I oftentimes felt like the adult chaperone in a room full of juveniles. Still, it was the best thing I had going for me at the time, so I did what I could to keep this so-called normal existence afloat.

By the summer of 1973, I had settled into a fairly regular routine of work, parties, dating and hanging out with the guys. Elvis had continued touring regularly; his "Aloha From Hawaii" album had hit Number One on the Billboard charts in May. The guy was on top of the world, and part of me longed to be there with him. So when he called me in August and invited me to spend a few days in Vegas, I didn't hesitate to take a vacation from work.

Elvis was at the Las Vegas Hilton for nearly a month, so I took a week to fly up there and enjoy time back in the familiar surroundings of the entourage. I guess deep down inside of me I knew that I would come back to this one day, but I really did want to try to make life work for me on my own terms. Invigorated by my time spent back in the world I once knew, I returned to Nashville just as Larry was starting his senior year in high school. It was the best of both worlds, I guess; I could live the life of a young adult, working on Music Row in Nashville by day, and having the freedom of being on my own at night. At the same time, I enjoyed the youthful pleasures that Larry and his buddies were reveling in throughout their senior year of high school. It was a good life, and I knew it. It was much different than the life I'd been living just one year earlier, and I was trying to appreciate every minute of it.

We were at a football game when I first noticed Angie. She was a cheerleader, a stunning girl with long legs and long brown hair. I literally stopped in my tracks the first time I saw her. Angie was tall, beyond pretty, and soon I learned, had a heart as beautiful as the body it lived in. I made sure that she was invited to the party at my apartment after the game.

When she walked into my apartment that night, the rest of the world disappeared. I was mesmerized and wasted no time in getting to know her--most of that night was spent talking only to her. She wasn't like anyone I'd ever met before, and she seemed less impressed by my association with Elvis than she was by who I was. My young heart immediately fell in love with her.

I had dated a lot of girls by this time, and had been with even more women, but Angie blew them all out of the water. She liked my ear for music, and we could talk for hours about what was on the charts. She was the whole package. Angie was everything I wanted a girl to be, and nothing like the ones I'd known up until then.

Her parents were cool too, letting me hang out at their house and even welcoming me. That was a first! I was consumed with Angie; I wanted to spend all of my time with her. If I wasn't at work, we were together, and I hoped that we would never be apart.

Our relationship grew stronger as the fall gave way to winter, so I took Angie home with me at Christmas. My family adored her, and they could see that she was a positive, calming influence on me. Mom was, of course, concerned that I was falling too hard too fast. But like everyone else, my mother also was glad to see that I seemed to be finding my way in this world. I knew that I wanted to marry Angie, that it would only be a matter of time.

Elvis had spent some time in the hospital in October and November, battling pneumonia and pleurisy, along with some other health issues. He had gained some weight by the time we saw him at Christmas, but seemed in good spirits and was eager to get back on the road. He was going to return to Vegas at the end of January. I wasn't entirely surprised when he called me just before Angie and I headed back to Nashville, asking me to go back on the road with him.

"I can't!"

"Yes you can, David," he responded. "Just come out like you did in August. You don't have to stay. Just come out and be with us for a little while."

The genie was pushing its way out of the bottle, but I still resisted.

"No, Elvis, I can't. I have a life here now. I have a job and Angie and an apartment ..."

"I miss you, David. I miss seeing you," he countered. "You need to come back. Come back to Memphis and work with me."

He knew that I had tasted the road, and he knew how hard it was to lose that taste. He also knew that I'd met a side of him that few people had seen, and it made sense to keep me close. Elvis could sense my hesitation over the phone.

"Come on, David. Just for a month. Come to Vegas."

"Let me talk to Angie," I begged, my resolve already fading.

"Alright, you do that. I'll see you in Vegas, David." I could almost hear the smile in his voice as I hung up the phone.

Angie was surprisingly cool with me leaving for the Vegas gig. She had no idea of what life was like on the road and, in her innocent mind, what could possibly happen in a month?

"It must be a blast," she said that night as she lay in my arms. "I mean, goin' to those concerts every night, meetin' all those stars – I've never even been to Las Vegas before!"

"Yeah, it's somethin', alright. Are you sure you don't mind me goin'?"

She gave that beautiful smile that always melted me inside.

"No, David, I told you – it's fine! I mean, I'll miss you, but it's only for a month, right?!"

I nodded, kissing the top of her head. I held an angel in my arms and felt the devil on my shoulder already beginning his victory dance. This time will be different, I promised myself. With Angie waiting for me at home, I knew that I could resist whatever temptations the road had to offer.

Tempted By the Fruit of Another

Things *were* different this time, mostly because I found myself playing a bigger role as one of Elvis' bodyguards. Being closer to the King meant being closer to the fans, and that, of course, put me closer to temptation. Elvis was obviously happy to have me back at his side, and I found myself constantly between the King and his adoring hordes of female fans. Maybe I hadn't been on the road for awhile, or maybe it was just because I had only been around high school girls for the past year, but these women seemed even prettier than they had when I was on the road before.

"Angie," I reminded myself. "Just keep thinking about Angie..."

I tried. I really did. And for the most part, I did a pretty good job.

Even though living on my own had made me grow up, the guys still considered me the kid of the group. That was probably the most frustrating part of being on the road. I went from being the "adult" with my peers at home to being cast into the role of child with the guys on the road.

We were back at one of the hotel suites, partying after our final Vegas show, when I slid out from under the brunette on my lap.

"I'm going to go get a beer," I told her. "Don't go anywhere, y'hear?"

She smiled back at me and I as made my way to the bar, Sonny grabbed my arm.

"Hey, boy, bring me one, too."

I was tired of being talked to like I was still a kid.

"Screw you, Sonny. I ain't your boy. Get your own damn beer!"

I shook his hand from my arm and angrily continued toward the bar. Everyone in the suite had heard the exchange – at least my part of it – and now all eyes were on me.

"David, come here a minute," Red said, glaring at me. He walked into the suite's adjoining room and stood there, his hand on the knob, waiting for me to join him. I remembered Elvis' admonition – *Don't mess with Sonny.* It looked like it was already too late for that. And now I was going to have to answer to Red. Sonny was much bigger than Red, but Red was as quick as he was hot-tempered.

I followed Red and he closed the door behind us.

"Whatd'ya want, Red? That brunette's waitin'..." I said, turning to face him. As I turned, Red's fist connected with my face and I stumbled backwards. I felt the all-too-familiar rush of blood over my face and instinctively put my hands to my face to quell the flow.

"Shit!" I looked at my hands, which were covered in blood. "Dammit, Red, what was that for?!"

"Boy, it's time you learned some manners," he said, walking toward me as I continued backing away. I'd never seen his face quite that angry before, and I had no idea what he had in store for me.

Elvis' suite lay just beyond a door on the other side of the room, and I made a break for it. As always, Elvis' handgun was on a table near the door and I grabbed it and had time to assume a menacing stance by the time Red made it through the doorway behind me.

"You stop right there, Red, or I swear, I'll blow your fuckin' head off."

Red stopped and we glared at each other, neither of us backing down from this fight, but both of us unwilling to make the next move. Red swallowed but said nothing.

"I'm serious, Red. I will blow your head off right here."

My chest was heaving with adrenaline, but my hands were steady, and I had Red's forehead squarely in the sights of my gun. He took a step backward, saying nothing as he realized that I meant what I said. After another step backward, he turned and walked from the room, closing the door behind him.

I lowered the gun, my body shaking with anger and fear. No longer in the mood to party with the crowd in the other room, I slipped out of Elvis' suite and returned to my room, alone. It was too late to call Angie and after I cleaned up my face, I laid on my bed, mulling over the insanity of the world I had semi-voluntarily rejoined. A knock on the door interrupted my thoughts.

"Hey, David, it's Red. Open up."

"No way, man!"

"Come on, David. Just open the door."

"Why? You gonna beat the hell outta me again?"

"No." He paused for a moment, waiting for the door to be unlocked.

"Come on, just open the damn door. I need to talk to you."

Finally convinced that he wasn't armed and wasn't there to kick my ass, I reluctantly let him in. He flinched when he saw my nose, which was swelling despite the ice-filled towel I was holding against it.

"Look, David, I'm sorry. I was outta line down there."

I knew how things worked in this game, and I didn't buy it.

"Yeah, right. Boss made you come here and apologize, didn't he?"

"Don't push it, David. I said I was sorry."

I looked at him, not yet ready to let bygones be bygones.

"Look," he continued, beginning to get irritated with me again. "You can't just be poppin' off like that. 'Specially in front of outsiders. It makes us all look bad."

"Look bad? Look what you did!" I shot back, pulling the towel away from my face.

"Alright, I admit I went a little overboard, but the intention was good..."

"I ain't the hired help, Red. I ain't nobody's boy and you know it. So why don't you guys quit treatin' me like I am."

He looked at me as if he'd just seen a ghost.

"What?" I asked.

"My God, you are just like your daddy."

"What? Why're you sayin' that? Ever since I was a kid, that's all I hear from you and Lamar – you're just like Bill Stanley."

"Well, it's the truth, David. He was one helluva guy, one helluva soldier. You know, to this day, I can't believe he didn't kill all of us."

I had no idea what he was talking about. His words caught my ears, as if he had waved one more piece of a missing puzzle in front of me. We had never really talked about Bill Stanley; I grew up calling Vernon "Daddy", and the few conversations I'd had with my mom were abrupt. He'd had a horrible drinking problem, she'd told me. That was just about all I knew about him.

"What are you talkin' about, Red? Kill who?" I demanded to know.

"Why don't you ask your mother?"

"What? Red – what the hell are you talkin' about?"
"Look, all I'm sayin' is – you got a raw deal. That's all."

He looked at me, realizing that he had said far more than he'd intended. He patted me on the shoulder as he turned to leave.

"Sorry about earlier, man. I mean it."

I hated talking about my father, didn't even want to think about it. Every time his name came up, it seemed like people got this look on their faces, like there was some big secret I wasn't supposed to know about. It haunted me, and I wished I could make all of it go away. It didn't matter if Bill had left us, I thought. We'd done just fine without him. But – what was Red talking about? Why would Bill have wanted to kill them?

Trying not to think about it, I opened another beer and lay back on my bed.

Elvis summoned me to his suite the next afternoon. My bags were already packed and I was ready to get back to my job and girlfriend in Nashville. Most of my time in Vegas had been a blast, but I was racked with guilt over my infidelity and I wanted nothing more than to be back with Angie.

"Hey, Boss, we're all ready to go – you wanted to see me?" I asked, popping my head into his suite. Elvis was sitting on the side of his bed, his little black "kit" open next to him. I could see the assorted bottles and vials inside and tried to ignore them.

"Whoa, Red really did lay into you, didn't he?"

I nodded, and Elvis motioned me to come closer so he could get a better look at the shiner I was sporting.

"He apologize?" Elvis asked.

"Yeah. Look, I ain't takin' none of their crap."

"Don't worry, David. It won't happen again. I straightened him out." He paused.

"So, you thought anymore about comin' on the road with me? I want you here, David."

"I told you – I got a job..."

"I'll handle RCA. You don't worry about that," he assured me.

"But I can't just leave Angie..."

"Then bring her with you! You two can move back to Memphis. That solves everything, right?

Elvis' way of solving things tended to only create more problems, and I knew it was pointless to argue with him.

"I'll think about it," I mumbled. He smiled and nodded, while I tried once again to stuff the genie back in the bottle before we boarded the plane to go home.

Back home, Angie was a welcome sight to me. I fell in love with her all over again, pushing memories from the road as far from my head as I could. I wouldn't leave her again, I swore it. Angie was everything that Elvis' world wasn't. She was pure, she was trusting, she loved me for me. She was the complete opposite of the women I met on the road, and I knew she offered the kind of stability my life needed. So when I left Nashville and moved back to Memphis, Angie came with me.

Our life together was fairly routine, at least as far as I was concerned. Angie loved animals – we quickly had more than a half-dozen cats – and she found a job working in a pet store. I started teaching at a karate school that Red and Elvis owned, and joined a band, playing the drums. My life was as good as it had ever been, and in April of 1974, I made Angie my wife.

We were married in a simple ceremony at the White Haven Church of Christ in Memphis, with about one hundred guests attending. There was no honeymoon, just a nice reception, then it was back to the apartment and our simple, but happy life.

Born to Run

The ink on our marriage license had barely dried when I got the call from Elvis, who was leaving on tour again. He had continued pushing me – hard – to come back on the road with him, and I had continued resisting. Angie was my wife, and my life was with her now. As much as I kept telling that to Elvis, it seemed like I was the only one who heard it.

"David, I'm leaving this evening. I want you to go with me," he insisted.

"I've told you, Elvis – I can't."

"Then just come meet me at the airport and say goodbye. Can you do that, David?"

"Uh, sure, okay. I guess we can."

He gave me his schedule and I promised to be there.

"Who was that?" Angie asked as I hung up the phone.

"Elvis. He's leaving tonight. He wants us to come to the airport and see him off."

She eyed me suspiciously. She knew how hard Elvis had been trying to get me back on the road.

"Are you sure thats all he wants?"

"I swear, baby."

The plane was waiting for us when we pulled up to the tarmac. Angie didn't move as I reached for my door handle.

"You comin'?" I asked her.

She shook her head.

"No, I'll wait here. Just tell him 'bye for me."

I smiled and nodded.

"I will, baby."

I leaned over and gave her a quick kiss on the cheek.

"I'll be right back."

I left the car engine running as I walked up the steps into the private Playboy jet Elvis was using for this tour. I stood in the doorway, looking at the familiar faces inside. There were several Playboy bunnies inside, all of them beautiful and none of them concerned about such technicalities as a wedding ring.

"David! Glad you could come!" Elvis said, a grin lighting up his face. "Come on inside. We're about ready to take off."

"I can't go, Elvis. Just like I said on the phone. I just came to say goodbye."

He put a firm hand on my forearm.

"Sure you can, David. It's only for a couple of weeks."

One of the bunnies came over to help persuade me. She wrapped herself around my other arm. I looked down at my waiting car, watching the look of horror on my wife's face. Elvis pulled me forward and pushed the door closed in one smooth move.

"Welcome back, David," he said with a smile. "It's good to have you."

I knew that I was a dead man walking. Most of my time on the flight was spent wondering how the hell I was going to get myself out of this one. I had been married less than two weeks, and I had just left my bride sitting alone at the tarmac watching a Playboy bunny wrap herself around me. There was simply no explanation that sounded good enough to cover that kind of transgression.

We went straight to Elvis' first concert of the tour. The concert seemed to last forever, and I called Angie as soon as I could get to a phone. She was mad, but not nearly as angry as I had expected her to be. Her voice sounded more hurt than angry, and that was worse.

"How could you just leave like that?" she wanted to know.

"It wasn't me, baby. I didn't have a choice..."

"But what about the girl..."

"Her? Come on. You know how the girls are on the road. They're just trying to be all friendly to get in good with Elvis. She didn't care about me, and nothin' happened."

"But David, you just left me."

"I'm sorry, Angie. I didn't wanna hurt you. I don't wanna be here. Look, I'll be home soon and we'll go back to how it was, okay?"

I think we both wanted to believe it. I knew that I wanted to make domestic life work for me, but I also knew that I had a wild streak in me that was fed every time I went out on the road. I wasn't sure which one would win.

Outside my room, I could hear a commotion in the hallway.

"Look, baby, somethin' is going on outside. I gotta go. I'll call ya later – I love you!"

I opened the door and could hear a woman's screams coming from Charlie Hodge's room. Ricky had heard the sounds from his room and was coming down the hallway from the other direction. We followed the sounds, curiosity turning to alarm as the woman's pleas grew louder. I didn't bother knocking when I reached the door. Shoving it open, I found a young woman fending off a very drunk Charlie.

"Charlie!" I yelled. "What the hell are you doin'?!"

Charlie had the young woman up against the wall. She was screaming and pleading with him to stop, but he seemed oblivious to the severity of the situation.

"Just havin' some fun, boys," he said with a laugh, looking in our direction briefly before returning his eyes to the girl.

"Please, stop him! Please!" the girl pleaded with us as we came closer. I grabbed Charlie's shoulder and pulled him away with enough force to knock him to the ground.

"Are you okay?" I asked the girl, who was only about eighteen years old. She nodded through tear-filled eyes and I held out my hand.

"Come on. Lemme get you outta here."

"Fuck you, man!" Charlie yelled at me while Ricky continued restraining him.

I led the girl to the elevator, past the security guards that were in place to keep unescorted fans from entering our floor.

"Ma'am, have we got a problem here?" one of them asked as we reached the elevator.

"No, sir," I assured him as I punched the appropriate buttons. "Just a little misunderstanding. Everything's fine."

He nodded, but continued watching us as we waited for the elevator to arrive. Once inside, I apologized to the girl.

"What's wrong with him?" she asked, her eyes again filling with tears.

Oh, God, I thought, please don't start crying again.

"Look, he's just drunk. He really isn't that bad a guy; he just had too much to drink, okay?"

She nodded, still shaken by the experience.

"I tell you what, if you can make the show tomorrow night, I'll have two front row tickets waiting for you. Okay?"

She looked at me and I saw her smile for the first time. She had a nice smile and I felt bad for her. I reached into my pocket and pulled out some money.

"Here, let me give you cab fare home, okay?"

"Thanks," she said as I stuffed the money into her hand.

"Is that enough?" I asked, not having the slightest idea as to how much money I'd just handed her. She nodded and as we reached the bottom floor, I made her repeat her name to me.

"Remember, two tickets for ya. Front row – tomorrow night. Okay?"

She was shaken, but giving a weak smile as she left the elevator. I made the ascent back to our floor, my anger welling up. What the hell was Charlie thinking?

Ricky was still in Charlie's room when I returned, trying to get Charlie to drink some coffee. Charlie was drunk and belligerent, and as Ricky slid a steaming cup of coffee across the table, Charlie knocked it to the floor.

"Charlie, what exactly is your problem, man?" I demanded as I walked into the room.

"Ain't no problem here, *boy*. That's none of your business."

"You're damn right it's my business," I said, my temper flaring. Ricky stood between us, hoping to diffuse the tension in the air.

"He's drunk, David. Let it go."

"Yeah, kid, let it go," Charlie snarled over Ricky's shoulder. "B'sides, I bet your little wifey would love to know 'bout all those broads you been bangin'."

It had already been a rough day, and this was icing on a cake that I didn't order. I picked up an ashtray and rushed past Ricky, smashing Charlie squarely in the face. Charlie recoiled from the blow, but quickly came back swinging.

Charlie was a little guy, maybe five-foot-seven on a good day, and he was no match for my size. Especially since he was drunk and I was stone cold sober. But if he was willing to give it a try, I was willing to give him whatever he had coming.

Charlie charged at me, his fists flailing madly. Ricky jumped in between us and I pulled my knee to my chest, putting all my weight into a sidekick that sent his slender frame flying backwards onto the bed. As Charlie took a swing at me, I blocked his punch and literally threw him into the hallway. He half-bounced, half-slid off the wall and I followed him through the doorway, jumping on top of him and pummeling him with my fists. It wasn't long before everyone on the floor seemed to be in the hallway, trying to stop me. The cops had been called from downstairs, and I swatted away the security guards like flies. Charlie was going to pay for what he said, and I was going to make damn sure of it.

"David! David! Stop it, son! You're killing him!" I felt Vernon's hands on my shoulders. I looked down at Charlie's bleeding face and rolled off him. My hands were dripping in blood... all Charlie's.

"Somebody call an ambulance," I heard Sonny say as Vernon hauled me back to my room. He slammed the door behind us, his face contorted in anger.

"Damn it, David, what has gotten into you?! You can't just go around beatin' up the help!"

"But, Daddy, he started it!"

"David, you could've killed him! And you probably would have!"

"Yeah, well he knew better than to bring Angie into it. He deserved everything he got."

"What's Angie got to do with this?"

I explained what Charlie had said, certain that Vernon would see my point of view as soon as he heard the entire story. Vernon sat silent for a moment and sighed.

"You know, David, maybe he's right. You ever think 'bout that? You're married now – maybe it's time you grow up, show a little self-control."

I couldn't believe my ears.

"Respect for my wife? Self-control? Me? What about..."

"You watch your mouth, boy," he spat back, his eyes ablaze. "Get those hands cleaned up and we'll finish this in the morning."

He stalked out of the room, slamming the door behind him. I was fuming, and there wasn't a single person I could talk to about it.

The first time I had met Vernon's girlfriend was on my first show in Vegas. She was an attractive woman by the name of Sandy Miller, and I got used to seeing her with him when we were on the road. Of course it was never brought up, that was the code of the road. What happened on the road didn't exist once we went back to our "normal" life at Graceland.

I was stunned and angered by what Vernon had just said. Just as his infidelity was a betrayal to my mother, his refusal to admit it was a betrayal to me. And throwing my own similar actions back in my face seemed both cruel and ludicrous.

Washing Charlie's blood from my hands, I discovered that my knuckles were bleeding from the beating I had just administered. I cleaned them up the best I could and sat on the end of my bed, wondering what I was doing here. Anyone else would have been fired on the spot, but not me. I knew that Elvis wanted me here. Even if I was a liability as far as everyone else was concerned, Elvis knew I'd always have his back. That alone was enough to save my job – even if it was a job I hadn't taken voluntarily and wasn't sure I wanted.

By the time I got to Elvis' room the next day, Vernon was already there. I knew he'd already told Elvis what had happened, so the best I could hope for was to get my side of the story in.

"Mornin', Boss," I said as I walked in, trying to act as casual as I could. My hands were swollen, and I tried to keep them out of sight.

"Daddy, excuse us," he said to Vernon, then turned to Red, who was eating breakfast.

"Get Charlie in here."

Both Red and Vernon eyed me as they left the room, and I knew I was in trouble – again.

"You got somethin' you wanna tell me?" Elvis asked, looking at me sternly.

"Yeah, I – uh – kinda got into it with Charlie last night."

"That's what I heard. David, you gotta learn to pull back sometimes. I pay these guys for a reason, ya know."

"But, Elvis..."

"Listen to me, David! The guys think you're a loose cannon. You're like a goddamn vigilante out there!"

I didn't have time to defend myself as the door opened and Charlie entered the room. Neither Elvis nor I were prepared for the sight. His head was swollen and bandaged, and he looked like he was wearing a hockey mask.

"You wanted to see me, Boss?" he asked, not looking at me. He was wearing sunglasses, but they couldn't hide the bruises and countless cuts across his face.

"Damn, boy! Come here, let me see."

Charlie did as he was told, removing his glasses to reveal bloody eyes surrounded by dark bruises. Elvis exploded.

"What the hell were you thinking?!" he shouted at me. I said nothing. I knew that Charlie had to be on stage with Elvis that night, and there was no way to disguise his temporary disfigurement.

"Out of here. Now!" Elvis snarled, pointing to his door. I saw no reason to argue. I walked silently to my room, thinking I didn't want to be on this damn tour in the first place.

Elvis didn't speak to me for three days, which meant that nobody else really talked to me either. After the shows I'd go back to my room and drink, talking to Angie on the phone and wishing I was back home with her. After three days of the silent treatment, I decided to take matters into my own hands, so I bravely marched down the hallway and into Elvis' room.

"I don't wanna talk to you," he said, looking up from his chair as I walked through the door.

"I don't care," I answered. "I wanna talk to you. What if you'd been married to Priscilla for ten days, and one of these guys on the road says as soon as they got home they're gonna tell Priscilla that you were bangin' everything alive?"

Elvis' eyebrows raised. Certain lines just weren't meant to be crossed, and this was one of them and I knew it was my only hope of redemption. Elvis picked up his phone and dialed Charlie's room. He calmly asked Charlie to come to his room – immediately.

Charlie came in, his head still showing the effects from our encounter, and he looked at me with the slightest bit of a smug grin.

"Hey, David, what's goin' on?"

"If you say another word to him, he's gonna kill you," Elvis said, looking directly at Charlie. "And you know what, Charlie? I'm not gonna stop him."

Charlie was clearly taken aback, shocked by the way the tables had suddenly turned.

"Don't push his buttons again, Charlie."

Charlie knew that he'd been out of line and that now Elvis knew what had caused our fight. It wasn't something to be taken lightly; the unspoken promise to keep the secrets of the road was among the strongest bonds we shared. Elvis cautioned Charlie about watching what he said, and Charlie seemed to take it to heart. It wasn't the last time Charlie and I would cross paths, but it was the last time Elvis jumped to the conclusion that everything was my fault.

Are You Looking for Trouble

At the moment Elvis slid the airplane door closed on that Memphis tarmac, I was reunited with him in every sense of the word. As hard as I had resisted going back on the road – and as determined as I was to make my marriage work – something inside of me clicked as the door of the plane locked into place. It was a private world that few people could understand, and an opportunity that even fewer would ever have.

On the road, as part of the King's entourage, we lived a life of constant access. Whatever it was that we wanted, we could have. It was like being a kid in a candy store, only we owned the whole store. I felt as if I was privileged enough to have been granted two lives that were playing out simultaneously. As much fun as I had on the road, I always looked forward to getting back home and seeing Angie again.

Between tours, Angie and I enjoyed a life that seemed idyllic. The moment that Elvis' private jet touched down in Memphis, I would once again become the faithful husband. The crazy thing was I did love her, but I had bought into the prevailing notion that what was being offered to me on the road was something I fully deserved to have. The cheating didn't hurt Angie, I reasoned, because she didn't know about it. It hadn't hurt any of the guys' wives as long as everybody kept their cool and stayed quiet about it. I didn't see why my marriage should be any different.

In Memphis, I served Elvis off the road in much the same way I did while on the road. Ricky, Dr. Nick's son Dean, Al Strada, and I would trade off shifts that ran in twenty-four-hour cycles. Someone was always on duty with Elvis, making sure that his needs were attended to. Whatever Elvis wanted to do during that shift was what I would end up doing. That meant that if Elvis wanted to go to the movies at night, I would call the film exchange and arrange for a private theater. If he wanted to ride his motorcycle, I'd call some of the other guys and round up a small group for that. Regardless of what he wanted to do, whether it was just lie by the pool or get out of town for the day, whoever was on duty made sure that he got to do it.

The Elvis that was revealing himself wasn't the same guy I had grown up with, or had even been on tour with a year earlier. Since I had been living in Nashville, I missed out on much of the trauma and drama of Elvis' life during late 1973. I knew from talk among the other guys that Elvis was having trouble dealing with some of the events that had shaped his life in the past couple of years. I knew that his divorce from Priscilla had hit him hard, and being separated from his daughter, Lisa Marie, was difficult for him as well. He had battled some health problems, but seemed, for the most part, to be doing better, yet his mood never seemed to return to quite the level of happiness that he had previously known.

We needed another show like his live Hawaii broadcast. "Aloha From Hawaii" remained his latest and greatest achievement and now, more than a year later, he needed another big show like that. We all needed it actually. We were beginning to see cracks in the armor. There was nothing wrong that we could really put a finger on, but it was obvious that Elvis wasn't nearly as on top of things as he had been. He was still selling out shows-- in Houston he set a one-day attendance record at the Astrodome with two shows, and back in Memphis he played four shows in two days to the sold out home crowd. If fans noticed that Elvis missed a note or a word here or there, they sure weren't showing it. They were as rabid as ever, and when we watched the crowds worshipping their King, it seemed as if this would simply go on forever.

When I wasn't on duty with Elvis, my biggest addiction continued to be martial arts. I practiced religiously, constantly striving to improve and working toward the next belt, and I also played racquetball with friends. Angie and I still met Elvis for movies every night as well. Angie was turning out to be the perfect wife, and was up for any adventure. Everyone liked Angie; she was beautiful and personable, and I knew that I was indeed a lucky man to have her. I slowly pulled her farther into my world though. The girl who didn't drink or smoke when we first married, would gradually have a daiquiri or a hit off a reefer.

By the end of May, we were at The Sahara Hotel in Lake Tahoe, where Elvis had an extremely fanatical following. The shows were so overbooked that management had to add additional shows, even going so far as to have a three a.m. show on Elvis' last day there. It was an exhausting time for all of us, and tensions were heightened in light of the social upheaval of the day.

Patty Hearst, granddaughter of publishing baron William Randolph Hearst, had been kidnapped in February, and in April the nation was shocked to see video surveillance tapes of her participating in a bank robbery. Elvis, always concerned for the well being of six-year-old Lisa Marie, became even more paranoid about his daughter being kidnapped. When Lisa Marie joined us for a week in Tahoe, we all stayed on high alert, driven as much by Elvis' anxiety as by our own concern for her safety.

Later that week, we had retired to the suite after the evening's shows and were having an uncharacteristically calm night. Elvis was in his room with Lisa Marie, watching news coverage of Patty Hearst and the SLA. I was passing time playing Pong in the suite, along with a couple of the other guys, when the electricity began flickering on and off, so I went to investigate. I walked through the double doors of the suite and into the hallway, and I could hear someone banging on the other side of the emergency exit door.

I pushed the door open and saw a man in a leisure suit, with a woman on each arm and a big, dopey grin on his face.

"Where's the party?!" he exclaimed loudly.

"There's no party here, buddy," I assured him. I saw the master switches on the wall near the stairs and realized that he had been flicking the switches. I looked down the hallway and motioned for the security guards to come help me.

"Listen, sir, you really need to leave. Elvis is in his room; he isn't taking any visitors. He's retired for the evening."

In a single motion, the man stepped forward and hit both of my shoulders – hard – with his outstretched palms. The force of his blows pushed me back against the wall and he continued coming toward me, angrily.

"Who the fuck do you think you are?" he demanded to know.

I came off the wall and was ready to unleash some anger of my own, but it was too late. Sonny had come to the doors of the suite and, the instant the man pushed me, he was on his way. He took the short distance in three long steps, winding up a right hook as he walked. Sonny's fist hit the man squarely in the jaw, and his head spun to the side, spewing teeth and blood into the hallway. Although the man was a good 260 pounds, the force of Sonny's punch was strong enough to lift him off the ground and send him flying into the wall.

"Far OUT, man! You tagged that son of a bitch!" I exclaimed, completely in awe of Sonny's strength. The man remained on the floor, stunned and shaking his head as his mouth bled and his entire face swelled. I returned to the suite and walked back into Elvis' room. He had Lisa Marie on his lap, a gun in each hand.

"What the fuck is goin' on out there, David?"

"There's this guy out there who tried to get in."

"Are you hurt?"

"No, Elvis, I'm fine. Sonny took him out."

"Show me!"

He put Lisa Marie down and followed me out of the suite. Red followed us into the hallway, but by the time we got there, the police had already taken the man to another room for questioning. The blood and teeth remained on the carpeting, and the women had fled.

"Sonny what happened?" Elvis wanted to know.

"The guy moved in on David, so I dropped him," Sonny explained.

"Where is the son of a bitch? I wanna talk to him," Elvis said. He was convinced the guy was trying to either kill him or get to Lisa Marie, and he wanted to do a little interrogation of his own. Sonny led us to the door he had seen the hotel security guards enter with the cuffed man in tow. Elvis opened the door, and we saw the man sitting on the end of a bed.

"What is goin' on in here?" Elvis said loudly, drawing the attention of the security officers as well as the man on the bed. "Is that the guy?"

"Obviously," I said, wondering how many guys just so happened to be sitting in a suite, cuffed and bleeding.

Elvis shook his head and sat down beside the man on the bed. Sonny and Red stood by the door, still angry, and I sat on the other side of the man, wondering if he was going to attempt to make a move on Elvis. Elvis looked at the guy, whose face was covered with his own blood, and I could see Elvis' anger melting.

"What are you doin', man?" Elvis asked, his voice soft and sympathetic. "What is your problem? You can't just come storming in some place and expect someone not to stop you. These guys are paid to protect me!"

The man didn't say anything.

"Is there anything I can help you with?" Elvis asked. The man looked up and saw Sonny standing before him, and the rage returned to his eyes.

"You son of a bitch!" he screamed. He leapt from the bed, his hands still bound behind him, and tried to kick Sonny. Sonny sidestepped the move, but Red immediately jumped in, landing a blow to the man's face and knocking him flat on his back.

"Goddamn, Red, what're you doing?" I asked incredulously. "You don't cap someone who's wearin' cuffs!"

"He was goin' after Sonny!"

"Doesn't matter! He was still in cuffs!"

Elvis and I knelt down on either side of him, and I could hear the blood gurgling in the man's throat. We picked him up and leaned him forward as the blood came gushing out of his mouth. The security guards escorted Sonny and Red from the room, and we stayed with him until he regained his composure. In the $6.3 million lawsuit he filed later that year, we learned his name was Edward Ashley and he claimed that he had been invited to a party after the show but was not allowed in. It did end up costing us some money, but in many ways, it was just the price Elvis paid for being the exalted King.

After Midnight

Elvis toured through June of 1974, then took some time off. Angie and I enjoyed a long summer together, and at night of the guys would come over to our apartment for cookouts and parties. While I was never going to hang out with the more straight-laced guys like Sonny and Red, there was a definite camaraderie with people like Joe Esposito and Lamar Fike. Sonny and Red looked at Billy, Ricky and me as kids, while Joe and Lamar seemed invigorated by our energy and saw our youthfulness as an asset. It was the same reason Elvis kept us around; they reveled in the infusion of pop culture and a hipper, younger attitude. So Joe, Lamar and my brothers became regular running buddies when we weren't traveling. We partied together, played together and rode Harleys together, never thinking about what our lives would have been like if we hadn't all been brought together by the musical greatness of a single man.

I played a lot of music when I wasn't on the road. Not only had I developed into a good drummer, but it was no small selling point to have Elvis Presley's stepbrother manning one of your instruments. As a result, I could play constantly, so when I wasn't on duty with Elvis, I was happy to sit in on the drums with a number of local bands. The music was exactly the opposite of what I was hearing on the road. I played mostly rock 'n' roll music with some blues influences thrown in for good measure. Songs by the Rolling Stones, BB King, Ike & Tina Turner, The Beatles, Led Zeppelin, America and Peter Frampton all made the set list.

The next best thing to being on a stage was being on the side watching one of my favorite bands performing live. Since I knew the building manager in Memphis, and usually knew either the promotion company or one of the crew members of a touring band, it wasn't a problem to show up and get in the back door. I'd met many of my idols this way, and although I wasn't exactly star-struck, I was still impressed by some of the talent I was shaking hands with.

Many of those rock stars had their own dream of meeting Elvis, and I was happy to help out when I could. When Eric Clapton's tour came through Memphis, he took advantage of the opportunity to meet Elvis. We were at the theater where Elvis was watching movies, when Jerry Schilling escorted an obviously humbled and impressed Eric Clapton into the theater.

Clapton had just returned to the music scene after kicking his heroin habit and reinventing his sound. Elvis knew who Eric Clapton was, and he also knew just how much Ricky and I adored him. So in true Elvis fashion, he decided to have a little fun at our expense.

"Elvis, I'd like you to meet Eric Clapton," Jerry began. Elvis shook Eric's hand.

"What're you doing in town?" Elvis asked politely.

"I'm doin' a concert."

"Where?"

"Over at the Liberty Bowl."

Elvis nodded.

"That's a big concert," he said admiringly. "What do you play?"

Ricky and I could not believe our ears. While we sat basking in the presence of the guitar god, Elvis was asking him what instrument he played!

"I-I play the guitar," Clapton explained, completely caught off guard.

"Are you any good?" Elvis asked. Ricky and I cringed.

Clapton seemed surprised, but not insulted as he explained that yeah, he was a pretty good guitar player.

"Tell you what," Elvis offered. "I can introduce you to my guitar player, James Burton. He'd probably be more than happy to give you a lesson or two."

Eric Clapton's eyes widened. But instead of anger or insult, we saw them fill with admiration.

"Really? That would be great!"

"Yeah, maybe I can get you two together and you can play a session," Elvis continued. Much to our surprise, Eric was excited by Elvis' offer. Ricky and I knew that Elvis was putting on this little show solely for our benefit. He wanted us to remember who he was, and this was the perfect reminder that, no matter what musicians we worshipped and listened to, those same musicians worshipped Elvis.

Of all the music that I listened to, Led Zeppelin remained my favorite band. We were out in Los Angeles when I got my first chance to meet them. Elvis was playing at the Los Angeles Forum, and I was out on stage before the arena filled up, making sure that his water, scarves and other personal stage necessities were all in the right place. As I stood on stage, I looked to my right and saw a man who looked remarkably like Robert Plant standing there. By the time I got off the stage he was gone, but I found Tom Hullett, who worked with Concerts West. As part of Concerts West, Tom and Jerry Weintraub had been brought in as Elvis' concert promotion company, and they also managed acts like Led Zep, Elton John and Paul McCartney.

"Did you see him?" Tom asked, grinning. My passion for Led Zeppelin's music was no secret.

"Yeah!" I answered. "Are you gonna bring them over?"

We were on tour, so instead of staying in Elvis' L.A. home, we were spending the night at the Hilton, which was across the street from the Forum.

"Sure, I'll bring 'em over," Tom promised.

I was thrilled. Of everyone I had met, this was the band that meant the most to me. I could hardly wait. I found Elvis backstage.

"Led Zeppelin's here!" I told him excitedly.

"Yeah, I know," Elvis responded. "Tom already said he's going to bring 'em over."

Ricky and I knew that Led Zeppelin was in town and might be at the show the night, so earlier that day we had gone to the record store and each bought another copy of their "Houses of the Holy" album. We both owned it, but wanted a copy for the band members to sign. Knowing that Tom had an "in" with the band, we were hopeful that we'd get the chance to meet them. Now it looked like my dream was going to come true.

114

Elvis had a great show at the Forum that night. It was the kind of show that made us believe in him all over again. When he went on stage and offered such a flawless performance, any fears that might have amassed during previous weeks or months suddenly seemed to instantly dissipate. At times like that, we knew that he was on his way back, and that his emotional and physical problems had been just a temporary setback.

I was in Elvis' room after the show and could tell that he was tired and wanted to be alone. I didn't want to miss the chance for the guys from Led Zep to come visit, so I reminded him that they were scheduled to meet him.

"Yeah, I know," he said, his enthusiasm waning. His incredible performance had obviously drained him. "Tell you what, David. I want you and Ricky to handle this."

I nodded. I left his suite and went out into the hallway, waiting for the elevator to arrive. It didn't take long until I heard the familiar "ping" and the doors slid open to reveal Robert Plant, John Bonham and Jimmy Page. If there was any disappointment, it was that John Paul Jones was not with them. I introduced myself and was over the top excited to meet them, particularly John Bonham. As a drummer, I had admired Bonham's handiwork from the first moment I heard him, and I had been looking forward to meeting the man whom I considered the world's ruling drummer.

As excited as I was to meet them, they were equally excited about meeting Elvis. I introduced myself and led them down the hall to Elvis' suite. I knew that although I would be happy to stay up all night with the band, I'd need to move them in and out of Elvis' suite fairly quickly.

I led them into the living room of Elvis' suite and told them to wait for me, then went into Elvis' room. Jerry Schilling, Joe

115

Esposito and some of the other guys were sitting around the suite chatting with Led Zeppelin, while I went into Elvis' bedroom and retrieved him. If he was tired or unenthused about meeting them, it didn't show. He walked into the room and said, quite unnecessarily, "Hi, I'm Elvis Presley."

I was no longer the most star-struck person in the room. The boys in the band seemed completely overwhelmed at meeting the rock icon that I knew so well. They introduced themselves and Elvis was his polite southern-boy self, telling them how pleased he was to meet them.

"I never picked up a guitar until I heard 'That's Alright Mama,'" Jimmy Page said. It was obvious that he was lost in his admiration for Elvis.

"Is that right?" Elvis said, and the smile on his face indicated he was pleased by what he heard. Any signs of strain from the evening's show seemed to disappear as he settled into the couch and began chatting with the guys. He had numerous questions for the band, as many questions for them as they had for him.

"So, do you guys party as much as I hear you do?" he inquired, and the boys grinned sheepishly.

"Oh, no, Elvis, it's not like they say," Robert Plant assured him. "It's all rumors. You should understand that."

Elvis smiled. "Oh, yeah. They're always talking about us, aren't they?"

A comfortable camaraderie settled over the room as the rock legends chatted, while Ricky and I excused ourselves to retrieve our new albums. The band was completely obliging and signed our albums without protest. In all the stars I had met – or would meet in the future – this was the only time I ever asked for an autograph.

I brought along stationery from the hotel as well, getting additional autographs from each of them. I didn't care if I looked like your typical fan, these guys were as good as it got, and I sure wasn't letting them get out of the room without getting their autographs.

They didn't stay long, as it was a courtesy visit on Elvis' behalf, and they understood that he wanted to unwind after pouring out his heart and soul on stage. They shook hands again and I began escorting them toward the door of the suite. Just as Robert Plant reached the door, he turned and began crooning, "Treat me like a fool..."

Elvis smiled. "...Treat me mean and cruel, but love me..." he joined in. The two men stood there, performing an impromptu acappella rendition of Elvis' song. The hairs on my arm stood up. It was a beautifully performed song and I wished then, as I have many times since then, that it had been caught on tape. The men finished their song, smiled at each other, and Led Zeppelin walked out of the door.

Our paths would cross again several times, but nothing ever erased the excitement of meeting them for the first time. I attended many of their concerts, getting backstage passes from Jerry Weintraub or Tom Hullett, and my passion for their music, to this day, remains unrivaled.

Toward the end of August 1974, we headed back to Vegas, enjoying about a four-week run at the Hilton. There was a marked difference between a regular tour and a Vegas show. On tour, we were flying from one city to the next, and these were often the kinds of tours we brought our wives along to enjoy. Sure, there were plenty of willing, screaming young ladies everywhere we went, but when you're in a different city every night, there just wasn't the time for exploits. Our schedule consisted either of arriving in town just before a show and leaving the next day, or leaving the same night, crashing in the hotel in the next city and spending the afternoon getting rested and ready for that night's show. It was a grueling schedule, and with this group, partying always took a back seat to the business of Rock 'n' Roll. I would party with the band, or sometimes with a group of people I met at the hotel, but there was a kind of control involved. Even as I let my hair down, I knew that the reason I was there was to get to the next city, and nothing would ever interfere with that.

Vegas, however, was a whole different ballgame. We would be there for weeks at a time, so everyone knew people who became part of our lives during our stay there. It was then that the wedding rings would come off and, with the exception of daily phone calls back home, the lives we had left behind at Graceland ceased to exist. I had begun seeing a flight attendant named Brenda, and she wasn't my only companion on the road, but she was certainly becoming a regular. I never really thought about how it affected my marriage because, honestly, my marriage stayed in Memphis. What happened on the road was completely removed from the life I had with Angie, and as long as I kept the two separate, I knew that everything would be just fine. Or so I told myself.

We were in Vegas when I met Alice Cooper for the first time. Cooper was there with Linda Lovelace, star of "Deep Throat," perhaps the best-known porn film of all time. All of the guys were giggling over Lovelace's presence there; we had passed plenty of jokes around beforehand, warning one another to keep their arms close and their legs tight or Lovelace just might swallow them whole.

Although I wasn't a huge fan of Alice Cooper's music, I had grown up with songs like "School's Out" and "Eighteen," and when I met him I found him to be incredibly intelligent. In fact, it quickly

118

seemed to me that he and Lovelace were an unlikely pair, as she didn't seem to be his intellectual equal.

Elvis was as polite and open to Cooper as he was to every musician he met. He always seemed more interested in what they had to say than in what they had to ask him about himself. Instead of talking about his own shows or music, Elvis asked Alice how his tour was going.

"Well, I've lost my python," Alice replied.

"Pardon me?" Elvis said, not sure that he had heard correctly.

"My python. I've got a twenty-foot python that's part of my stage show," he explained. "But somebody stole it. Now I've lost my python."

Without missing a beat or cracking a smile, Elvis asked him, "Well, did you ask Linda if she might know where it went?"

There was a moment of silence as we all sat there, knowing what we had just heard but not truly believing that Elvis had just said that. We watched Alice to see what his reaction would be, and as his face broke into a smile the rest of us burst out laughing. Fortunately, Linda Lovelace joined in the laughter as well.

I continued meeting rock stars that admired Elvis' work, and I often found myself face-to-face with people whose work left me in awe. I had listened to Elton John for years, and his tenth album, *Caribou*, had come out in January of 1974. It was a terrific album, with songs like "The Bitch is Back" and "Don't Let the Sun Go Down on Me." When he came backstage to meet Elvis, I was thrilled to shake his hand. It was a brief encounter; Elton basically had time to shake Elvis' hand and leave. As he walked away, Elvis turned to me and asked, "Isn't that the guy who wrote that song, 'Don't Let Your Son Go Down on Me?'"

"Elvis – that's THE sun. Don't let THE sun go down on me," I said, exasperated with a horrified look on my face. Elvis began laughing. He knew the name of the song, he just enjoyed jerking my chain. He teased me about the music and artists I listened to, but he was always respectful to them as artists. Elvis liked getting my goat, and making fun of the music I listened to was one of the best ways to do that. He was a true big brother in every sense of the word.

It was also a way to remind me of who I worked for. He wasn't jealous of other artists, but he often didn't appreciate my enthusiasm for the kind of rock music that was dominating the charts in the early to mid-seventies. I put back stage pass stickers of bands I'd seen or liked on my brief case, and one day he noticed a new sticker that both caught his attention and raised his ire.

"What's that?" he asked, pointing to the offending object.

"That's my KISS sticker," I explained.

"Well, kiss my ass and get it off of there," he said.

"Why?"

"Look at the bottom of your paycheck. See who signs it. That's all the explanation you need."

Elvis wasn't trying to be mean about it, but he was trying to teach me a lesson. He wanted me to remember whom I worked for and where my loyalties were. It was so easy, in the midst of such stardom, to get distracted by the hot, rising acts of the day. I was meeting heroes of mine on a regular basis. Elvis didn't agree with my musical tastes, but his words had nothing to do with that specifically. He only wanted to remind me what we were all working for. It wasn't just a business, it was a lifestyle, and it was a family. Elvis wanted to make certain that it stayed intact.

Not that he had to worry. As enamored as I was with the rock 'n' rollers I met, I knew there was a reason they all called Elvis The King. Every time he walked on stage, it was a reminder that there was only one Elvis Presley. Nobody ever captured the kind of presence he had. I saw hundreds of concerts during my youth, and more than a thousand Elvis performances. Elvis, even on a bad night, surpassed most bands I ever saw on stage, and that holds true to this day.

The difference, I guess, is that I was a fan of the other rock bands. I couldn't say I was an Elvis fan per se. I was more of a respecter of his music. Even if it wasn't what I would choose to listen to in my own time, I had a deep appreciation for what he was doing and a tremendous sense of awe for the way that he was able to do it. And as much as I dug the other musicians I had met, I always knew that my place was at Elvis' side. He was family, plain and simple.

On this trip, our stay in Vegas was less than a month, and Elvis was spending less and less time with us after the shows. Where he initially partied with everyone else after the shows, that was changing by the end of 1973. He had started turning inward after his divorce, but now his health was beginning to affect his mood as well. He was beginning to look tired, and he seemed more eager just to retreat to his room after his performances. In some ways, it made our jobs easier; we could make sure he was in for the night, then go do whatever kind of partying we had planned. But it was becoming more and more obvious that whatever was up with Elvis, wasn't going to go away on its own.

After Vegas, we were home for a couple of weeks, then went back on the road for another two weeks. We were playing in Cleveland when I met another rocker I liked, John Anderson, lead singer of the band Yes. Elvis was appearing at the Coliseum, and Yes was doing an outdoor concert in the football stadium. We arrived in Cleveland at around ten o'clock, and I noticed the billboards advertising Yes' concert the following night.

After we had gotten Elvis settled into his room, I wandered down to the lobby and saw a huge crowd. It wasn't the traditional throng of Elvis fans, these were rock 'n' rollers. And, from the looks of the concert t-shirts they were wearing, this crowd was here to catch a glimpse of Yes.

I inquired at the front desk as to whether or not Yes was staying there, and when the night manager confirmed that they were, I asked if I could leave a note. The manager slid a piece of paper across the desk and handed me the pen.

"Dear John," I wrote to John Anderson.

"My name is David Stanley. I'm the stepbrother of Elvis Presley and a big fan of yours. I'd love to meet you."

I signed off with my room number, then headed back up to Elvis' suite to see if he needed anything from me. We were hanging out, just talking, when the phone rang. Elvis answered it and then, looking puzzled, handed it to me.

"This is the hotel operator," the voice on the other end of the line informed me. "I have a message that I've been asked to give you."

She then told me John Anderson's room number and told me that he wanted me to call him. I was excited! I was a huge Yes fan and thought Anderson's ethereal vocals were absolutely incredible.

"Elvis, are you done with me? I gotta go," I informed my boss after I hung up the phone.

"Where you goin'?"

"I'm...uh, I'm going to meet a friend."

"Who?"

"It's a band called Yes."

Elvis looked puzzled. "Yes? What the hell kind of name is that?"

"I don't know," I shot back. "But the guy's name is John Anderson and he left a message for me to call him. Do you need anything else?

"No, go ahead, I'm fine," Elvis assured me. "I'm gonna head to bed anyway."

I hurried to my room and called John, who asked me to come down to his room. When I got there, he had a couple of bottles of wine sitting on the table and explained to me that he was working on a solo album. He poured me a glass of wine and I sat across from him, breaking the ice with the familiar shop talk. Unlike almost all of the rock stars I had met, Anderson was not a big Elvis buff. He respected Elvis' greatness, but, like myself, didn't find that the music fit well within his rock 'n' roll repertoire. I found his presence calming; he was surprisingly soft-spoken and had a gentle demeanor that seemed to fit perfectly with the relaxing effects of the wine.

We talked for a few minutes about Elvis, and after he had asked a number of questions about working with the King, I asked him about his own tour.

"It's good," he said, looking genuinely happy about it. "You should come over to the stadium tomorrow. You can hang out with us and go to the show."

I wanted nothing more than to leap at his offer, but knew that I would already have a busy day tomorrow getting ready for

Elvis' show. There was no way that Elvis would let me out of duty just to go see a rock band perform. Especially one he had never even heard of. These were the times when the responsibility of rock 'n' roll overshadowed its glamour; instead of hanging out with Yes, I'd have to spend my day working. However, when you considered whom I was working for, I suppose I didn't really have a lot of room to complain.

Politely explaining my situation to John, I regretfully had to decline his offer. We continued drinking the wine, and he played me a few songs he was working on. It was a surprisingly tame evening, and we didn't meet again until after Elvis' death. The next time I saw him was 1978 and Yes was playing in Memphis. I showed up at the arena and he took me backstage with him. I had brought along one of the extra "TCB" necklaces that Elvis had given me. Elvis was notorious for giving away things that belonged to other people, and when he gave me a second TCB necklace, I figured that I might as well hang onto it, because you never knew when he was going to offer yours to someone else. For some reason, the time I spent with John in his hotel room in 1974 made an indelible impression on me, and I presented him with the spare TCB necklace. Perhaps he seemed like the perfect person to own it because he was more like me – not a rabid fan, but definitely an appreciator of what Elvis accomplished.

We were back in Memphis for the last couple of months of 1974. His shows during October were mixed at best. A good performance would be followed by a rambling, sometimes incoherent Elvis. He was canceling shows on a whim, and we were having trouble getting him on the stage in time for other shows. He walked off the stage a couple of times in Vegas, and we were spending more and more time worrying about what would happen once we got him on the stage. Elvis was gaining weight, going from a trim 168 pounds to around 175-180. I found myself making more frequent trips to the pharmacist, picking up drugs ordered by Dr. Nick, and on the nights when I was on duty with him back in Memphis, I noticed that the number of sleeping pills he was taking at night was increasing at an alarming rate.

The Elvis I had known for 14 years was fading right before my eyes. The man in his place was pleasant and friendly, but nothing like the god-like creature I had grown up with. Although the wheels weren't falling off the bus just yet, they were certainly becoming wobbly. As bad as things were then, I couldn't even fathom the level of despair that was about to ensue.

Is There a Doctor in the House

By the end of 1974, Elvis was showing strains of being on the road non-stop, and I had to admit that the rest of us weren't looking so hot either. He had performed two extended Vegas engagements, and had done two Lake Tahoe runs for a total of more than 150 shows, and we had maintained a rigorous schedule on the road beyond that.

During our second leg of shows in Las Vegas, Elvis put his health care in the hands of a doctor named Elias Ghanem. Dr. Ghanem was something of a celebrity doctor in Vegas, and had first treated Elvis a couple of years earlier. Now, whenever we were in Las Vegas, Elvis relied on him for treatments – all in addition to whatever Dr. Nick was doing. Elvis had a doctor in every port, and when Ghanem told Elvis about a new "sleep diet" he had created, Elvis was ready to listen.

With his fortieth birthday just around the corner, Elvis' spirits were slumping. It seemed that everyone, from the *National Enquirer* to Johnny Carson to the Nightly News with Walter Cronkite were talking about Elvis being "fat and forty." He had been working hard to get a movie project, "New Gladiators," off the ground. The documentary, which Elvis financed, would feature Ed Parker and members of the U.S. Karate Team. They had also filmed more than thirty minutes of Elvis doing karate, but he was unhappy with how heavy he looked on film and wanted to re-shoot his segments.

On a brisk December night, Elvis called me at the apartment and said we were going to Vegas. I had no idea what he had in mind, but he sounded like he was in good spirits, so I figured this would be more pleasure than business. Within a couple of hours, the plane was ready and heading to Vegas with Ricky, Billy Smith, Al Strada, Elvis and me.

When we landed at a private airport, a light mist was falling and the lights bounced off the runway in a soft glow. I watched out the window as three black Mercedes-Benzes pulled up on the tarmac. There was a lot of fun to be had in Vegas, and I was more than ready to cut loose and enjoy it.

As the door of the plane opened, I saw Dr. Ghanem walking up the steps.

"What are you doin' here?" I asked, completely surprised to see him.

"I'm here to pick up Elvis," he replied, walking past me onto the plane. Elvis heard the doctor's voice as he entered.

"Come on back, doc!" he hollered. "I'm back here."

We had no idea what was going on, but we knew enough not to ask questions. After about twenty minutes, Dr. Ghanem emerged from Elvis' room at the rear of the plane.

"He's gonna need some help," the doctor said as he left the plane. We looked at each other, not sure what had happened or what his comment meant, but I think we all had a sneaking suspicion.

"I guess it's time to go," I said, finally. "I'll go get Elvis."

When I walked into Elvis' room, I was shocked to find him completely unconscious. I could feel my heart begin racing as I tried to get him to respond, and was relieved just to find a pulse.

"Ricky! Al! Get back here!" I shouted. "I can't wake him up!"

We realized that he was out for the night, and, together, we dragged him down the steps of the plane into one of the waiting cars. Dr. Ghanem was there, waiting. We were told that we were going to his house for the next three days.

There, I would learn, Dr. Ghanem had built what he called a special suite to treat patients on his sleep diet. Basically, he hooked Elvis up to an IV to keep him hydrated, but he also kept Elvis so drugged that he didn't wake up. It was a brutal few days, with the four of us taking turns cleaning up Elvis' bodily functions and sitting around the house killing time. In addition to being a complete waste of our time, the three days of unconsciousness did little, if anything, to help Elvis' ballooning weight.

He celebrated his fortieth birthday quietly, and we were all looking forward to returning to Vegas for a run of shows beginning in late January and running through early February. It was obvious to most everyone that Elvis wasn't ready for the gig. Even though he kept talking about getting in shape for the shows, he was bloated and lethargic, and within days of his birthday, Col. Parker sent out a press release announcing that the Vegas shows had been rescheduled for March. So much for the sleep diet.

Inside the house, it felt like things were falling apart at the seams. We kept waiting for the magic bullet that would bring Elvis back, hoping for that day when the old Elvis returned triumphantly. On January twenty-ninth, he was admitted into the hospital after Elvis' labored breathing awakened his girlfriend at the time, Linda Thompson. Struggling just to pull air into his lungs, Elvis was rushed to the hospital, and for the next two weeks, we took up residence there as well. What others called "fatigue," we called "detox." We just hoped that this time it would take.

Elvis lost ten pounds during his hospital stay, which lasted until Valentine's Day. During that time Vernon had a heart attack, and it landed him in the ICU for a few days, and he had the room right next to Elvis. Everything seemed shaky and uncertain, like we suddenly were living day-to-day, not really sure where all of this was headed. And when I wasn't at the hospital, I had plenty to occupy my mind.

My mom had long suspected that our life on the road was far from wholesome, but as problems escalated in her marriage to Vernon, I suddenly found myself caught in the glare of her spotlight as she searched for concrete answers. I had known Vernon's girlfriend, Sandy Miller, since my first or second engagement in Vegas, but it was another part of life on the road that I just had learned to accept.

From the time I went on the road with Elvis, my relationship with my mother had changed. In retrospect, there was very little interaction – I answered to Elvis on the road, and when I came home, I pretty much lived my own life. My life was on the road with Elvis, or at home with Angie. Now, however, mom was desperate to find some information that would either confirm or put an end to her suspicions, and she was causing problems for all of us.

"We've got to talk about Vernon," she said to me one day when she happened to catch me alone in a room at Graceland.

"Mom, I don't have anything to say," I protested.

"Well, you have to know something, David. You're out there on the road with him. You have to know what's going on."

I knew plenty, but I certainly wasn't in a position to fill her in on it. I had my own fairly constant companion, Brenda, who was a flight attendant on the private jet that we traveled on. When I became part of Elvis' inner circle, I automatically assumed the code of the road – I would cover Vernon's ass, and he would cover mine. Indiscretions and infidelities stayed on the road, and were never referenced to anyone outside our circle. Not even my mother could trump that.

One of the guys had once told me, "Never get high with anyone unless they have as much – or more – to lose as you do." Those became words to live by, and it applied to every aspect of my life. All of us on the road were guilty of cheating or worse, and because we all partook, we all could trust one another for protection.

"It's none of my business!" I countered.

She looked at me, stunned and disappointed. She knew that I knew something and I could tell that she felt my loyalty to Vernon was a direct betrayal of her. To me, it truly wasn't any of my business. Her problems with Vernon had nothing to do with me, and, as Elvis would say, "That's their baby, let them rock it."

As tensions between Mom and Vernon mounted, they separated and Vernon moved out. He had already moved Sandy into a house around the corner, but he continued taking care of Mom financially, until their divorce was final in 1977.

Elvis felt bad about the whole thing and bought my mom a brand-new baby blue Cadillac. But he also wondered what kind of effect it would have on us working with him. Ricky and I were wondering the same thing, and when he summoned us to Graceland after we'd learned about the separation, both Ricky and I were nervous. We didn't know what Vernon's separation from our mother would mean for us, and when we went to Elvis' room, we found him in a serious mood.

"Boys, I want to talk to you about this," he began. I tried to imagine what I would do if I weren't working for Elvis. I was only making about $275 a week, but everything in my life, with the exception of my rent, was paid for. I could never live on a regular income the way that I lived on Elvis' payroll. And, more importantly, I couldn't imagine doing anything else – or working for anyone other than Elvis.

"What's the deal with Vernon and Dee?" Elvis asked. "How do you boys feel about everything? What I want to know is – will this have any effect on our relationship?"

Ricky and I exchanged a look of relief. Elvis seemed just as worried about losing us as we were about losing him.

"Listen, Elvis, I work for you," I began. "I am loyal and dedicated to you. Whatever's happenin' with Mom and Vernon – that's their lives and it's none of my business. I guess the bigger question is, how do you feel about it?"

Elvis looked at us and smiled that slow, perfectly crooked smile.

"I love you guys," he said. "You do a great job and I love having you with me. That's all that matters."

It was a huge relief to hear those words, and not just because it meant that Ricky and I still had jobs. I had always wanted to believe that we meant something to Elvis, that we weren't there out of some sense of obligation.

With our parents in the early stages of divorce, Elvis was proving that we were more than just part of a package deal that came with Dee; we had become a part of his life. Above and beyond the fact that we had been joined by our parents' marriage, we truly were brothers and friends.

Initially things were a bit awkward with Vernon waiting to see how Ricky and I would react to him. It wasn't as if we hadn't been around Sandy all these years, but that was different. Then, it was just part of the secret life on the road. Now it had become something very real and had intruded on the life Vernon lived back home. He approached me one day to make sure that there would be no hard feelings.

"David, I want to say something about me and Dee ..." he started, obviously uncomfortable with the words even as they left his lips.

"You don't have to, Daddy," I answered. "I don't care. That isn't my problem."

I didn't want to talk about it and, the truth was, I didn't care. It didn't make any difference to me now. I had a marriage of my own to worry about and most of the time I lived in such a state of denial that I didn't want anything to shake me out of it. I was in denial about the life we lived on the road, in denial about how it affected my marriage, and in denial about the downward spiral that Elvis was on. This was the way that everyone else around me kept up the façade of the life we lived, and I had learned it well. Keeping this charade alive was our only hope of survival.

Elvis' Las Vegas shows were re-scheduled for March. In the month or so after he was released from the hospital, he spent time in the recording studio and he also began playing racquetball again, trying to lose some of the extra weight he was still carrying. When the Vegas show opened on March eighteenth, Elvis was still bloated and struggling with his weight, so he made jokes about it as part of his act.

Although initial reviews of the show were good, the performances after opening night were a roller coaster ride. He often seemed exhausted, and what once had been on-stage patter with the crowd now turned into long, rambling, often unintelligable monologues. Elvis would forget the words to his songs, and while he sometimes would cover up his mistake with a good-natured smile and a joke, at other times he simply grew frustrated.

Less than halfway through his Vegas run Elvis was having a particularly bad night. I was standing in my normal spot on the floor, between the audience and the stage, and I could see Elvis' frustration boiling into anger. The crowd was growing impatient with him and he seemed completely disoriented. I looked over to the side of the stage, where Sonny and Red were watching over him. The looks on their faces mirrored the concern in my own.

Elvis tried to regain his composure, but seemed dazed and drugged. Finally, as we watched in disbelief, he put down the microphone and left the stage. I saw him storm past Sonny and Red, who turned and followed him. As the crowd began to boo, I jumped onto the stage and raced to catch up with Elvis, Sonny and Red.

Elvis was walking quickly and forcefully, completely ignoring Sonny and Red.

"Boss, you can't do this," Red implored. "You gotta get back out there..."

"The hell I do," Elvis spat back, pushing open the door to his dressing room. As to door swung open, Vernon and Lamar looked up from the dressing room couch.

"What the hell?..." Vernon began. Elvis stormed past his father, not answering as he entered his private dressing room, slamming the door behind him.

"Son?" Vernon called out, rising from the couch with a bewildered look on his face. He turned to face Sonny, Red and me. "What the hell happened?"

Sonny was as mad as I'd ever seen him, and I had seen him plenty mad before.

"He walked off the damn stage. Can't even remember his own fuckin' songs, that's what happened."

Lamar released a heavy sigh. "Lemme go get the doc."

"Fuck the doc!" Red shouted, angered by Lamar's suggestion. "Dammit, Lamar, don't you see that doc's the problem?!"

The two men faced off, angrily staring each other down. Vernon stepped in between them.

"Now, hold on, boys," he said. "Everybody just settle down and let's think this thing through."

Sonny stepped forward, still seething.

"No, Vernon, you know Red's right. Somebody's gotta get some balls around here. Nobody'll tell him 'no' – that's the damn problem!"

It was like watching my family fight, watching them tear into one another out of anger, frustration and fear. I stood there, witnessing the fight in front of me and still able to hear the booing of a disappointed crowd in the background. We knew the shows in Vegas weren't going well, and that had created tensions between Elvis and the band while on stage. But none of us were prepared for him to just walk out like that. Elvis had always taught me that we did this for – and because of – the fans. Now it seemed that the drugs had gotten the best of him and were making him break his own cardinal rule.

Unwilling to drop the matter, Sonny and Red headed toward the door Elvis had slammed just moments earlier. Without knocking, Sonny pushed it open and I could hear Elvis growl, "What the hell are you lookin' at?"

"Boss, you gotta get a grip," Red started. "Put the pills down. I mean it."

"Get out!" Elvis shouted back.

"You can't keep going like this, man! Have you looked at yourself?"

"I said get out! Ain't none of your goddamn business," Elvis screamed.

Sonny pushed forward, past Red.

"Listen to them!" he yelled, gesturing toward the open door where the fans' disappointed chants and boos lingered. "It's their business! You're on stage for half an hour and then walk off? What the fuck are you thinkin'?!"

"To hell with them," Elvis said. "Get Dr. Nick."

Red stepped in, trying to calm down the two men.

"Boss, look, we're just worried about ya. Man, you gotta slow down with this shit. You're just takin' too much shit. Don't you think you've had enough?"

"Who do you think runs this goddamn show, Red?!" Elvis yelled. "Have you looked at whose autograph is at the bottom of your check?"

Red fell silent.

"Yeah, that's right," Elvis said. "I'll decide what's enough."

I looked at Vernon, who was listening nervously to the heated exchange. He didn't have any more ideas than I did as to how to stop this speeding, wreckless train that was hurtling toward a fiery crash. Sonny jumped in to try and defend his cousin.

"Come on, man – Red's right! You're doing too goddamn many drugs!" he shouted. "I've known you for twenty years, and you're turnin' into nothin' but a fuckin' drug addict."

"Get out!" Elvis commanded. "Get outta my room!"

The main door opened and Dr. Nick entered, followed closely by Lamar. As they headed toward Elvis' room, Red and Sonny stormed out of it.

"Fuck it, man. It's your funeral," Sonny yelled over his shoulder.

I shook my head in disbelief.

"This is all your fucking fault," I told Dr. Nick as he pushed past me. "You know that, don't you?"

He didn't say a word, but simply closed the door behind him as he got down to business. It was a grim evening, and it wasn't the last night we'd have like that in Vegas. Elvis walked off the stage about three times during the Vegas Hilton engagement, and tensions within the band continued to mount. I coped with it the only way that I knew how – by smoking reefer and blowing cocaine. I'd wash it down with beer or scotch and just hope that the next day would be better. I watched Elvis dance with his demons, but paid little attention to my own. I didn't know how that was going to happen, but I knew that something needed to change – and soon.

Ricky, Billy, David and Vernon at Graceland - 1960

Vernon Presley and Dee Stanley's Wedding - 1960

Vernon and Mom at Graceland - 1960

Elvis and David at MGM Studios - 1967

Billy, Ricky, David and Elvis - 1967

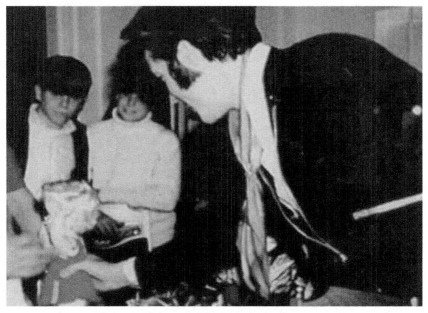

Billy, David and Elvis - Christmas - 1968

Elvis and David in Las Vegas - 1972

Elvis and David (far right) On Tour - 1973

Elvis and David in Las Vegas - 1974

Elvis, David and Dr. Elias Ghanem in L.A. - 1974

Elvis and David (far right) On Tour - 1974

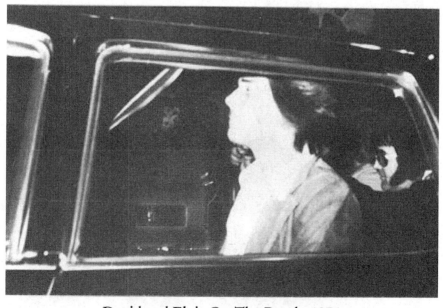

David and Elvis On The Road - 1974

Elvis and David Doing a Karate Demo - 1974

David (front of plane) and Elvis On Tour - 1975

Elvis and David On Tour - 1975

Elvis and David On Tour - 1975

Elvis and David (far right) On Tour - 1976

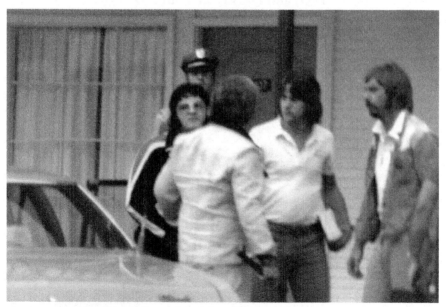

Elvis and David (white shirt) On Tour - 1976

Elvis and David On Tour - 1976

Elvis and David On Tour - 1976

Elvis and David On Tour - 1976

Elvis and David On Tour - 1976

David, Elvis and Joe Esposito leaving The Stage - 1977

Elvis, Joe Esposito and David On Tour - 1977

Elvis and David (far right) On Tour - 1977

Elvis and David (leaning over) in Hawaii - 1977

Elvis, David (white pants) and the guys in Hawaii - 1977

Elvis and David On The Road - 1977

Elvis and David On Tour - 1977

Elvis, David (left) and Joe Esposito On Tour - 1977

Elvis, David and Joe Esposito On Tour - 1977

Elvis and David On Tour - 1977

Elvis and David On Tour - 1977

Elvis and David On Tour - 1977

David, Angie and Linda Thompson at Elvis's Funeral - 1977

Look Into My Father's Eyes

We stayed in Vegas until April first, then went back home before launching a tour at the end of April. This time, the problems of the road didn't stay on the road. For years, I'd had trouble sleeping; I was plagued by nightmares about being separated from my father and now I was just as troubled by what was happening with Elvis.

Sleeping became impossible without help from a joint or a few drinks, and even then, I'd wake up in the middle of the night unable to fall back asleep. There was a heavy feeling of uncertainty that hung over me, and when I would wake in the middle of the night, I felt as though that uncertainty and anxiety completely consumed me.

I had too much on my young mind, and it was only in the dark of night, when everything was quiet, that it had the chance to get my attention. Angie tried her best to understand what was going on, but I wasn't much for answering a lot of questions, and she was getting tired of asking.

I was staring out the window, smoking a joint one morning about four a.m. when Angie woke up.

"David? What're you doin'? What time is it?"

"I dunno. It's late, I guess. Go back to sleep – I'll be there in a minute."

She sleepily pulled herself from our bed and came over to sit beside me.

"What is it David? Another dream about your dad?"

I shook my head.

"No, not this time. It's just – this shit with Elvis, man. I don't know what's goin' on. I don't know what's going to happen. I'm startin' to get worried about him, and so are the other guys. But you can't tell him a damn thing."

She listened quietly, as I said out loud the same things all of us had been thinking for months. We could see the rapid deterioration, and I found it so hard to believe that only two years had passed since he had charmed the world with "Aloha From Hawaii." His drug use had increased right after Priscilla left, but he did rebound for a bit. Now it seemed like he was getting worse than ever and I feared that everything was on the verge of falling apart.

"How long 'til the next tour?" she asked, knowing that it was nearing but uncertain of the dates.

"About two weeks. But we'll only be out a couple a weeks."

She sighed.

"What if you didn't go, David? What if this time, you stayed home instead of going out with them?"

"And do what?" I looked at her incredulously. "My life is with Elvis. He needs me."

"And what about what I need? Do you ever think of that?"

158

My haunted reflection was giving way to rage.

"Cut it out, Angie. You knew what you were getting into when we got married."

"Did I, David? Did *you* know what we were getting into?"

"What the hell are you talking about?"

"Us, David. Or you. You never talk to me anymore. It's like if you're here, you wanna be on the road. You can't stand to be home anymore."

"Baby, that's not …"

"It is true, David, and you know it! Even when you're here, you're like some robot or something. I don't even know who you are anymore!"

I gave a heavy sigh. I didn't know who I was anymore, either. Hell, there wasn't much of anything I *did* know at that point. I only knew that I had a job to do, and that job was with Elvis. He would always be my first priority.

I waited until I thought she had fallen asleep before I crawled back into bed. I lay next to my wife, our bodies not touching, wishing sleep would take me away from all of this. The sad truth was, she was right – I didn't want to be home. The road had become my home and I now felt restless after more than just a few days in one place. But I also knew that I didn't want her to leave. I couldn't imagine my life without her, but couldn't fulfill my promise of a life with her.

I stared at the ceiling until my eyes finally grew heavy and I found myself in a blissfully unaware state of unconsciousness. I could see my father, Sgt. Bill Stanley, standing before me in his military uniform. He was young again, and instead of the pain of loss etched across his face, he wore of look of compassion and love.

"You'll never be alone, David. Never," he said. I watched as a door suddenly appeared between the two of us and then slammed shut.

"Shit!" I screamed, bolting upright in bed. Angie instinctively jumped up and reached for me.

"David! What is it?"

"Fuck! Another dream. Nothin'. Just go back to sleep."

I angrily yanked back the covers and strode to the window, rummaging around for the joint I'd put out less than an hour earlier. Angie sat quietly in the darkness, her face briefly illuminated by the flash of my cigarette lighter.

"Your dad?" she asked.

I took a long hit and held it, grateful for the smoke that was filling my lungs.

"Yeah," I said as I exhaled. "Sgt. Bill again."

"David, why don't you just call him? You might feel better."

"Go back to sleep, Angie. I'll be there in a minute."

I wanted the whole world to stop. I wanted to reach inside my heart and pull out every bit of pain that filled it. I wished I could find some answers to the questions that I didn't know how to ask. But mostly, I just wanted to stop feeling.

Elvis was touring in Florida that spring, so I decided to call my father and invite him to come out to the show. Elvis was constantly encouraging me to have some sort of reconciliation with

160

Bill Stanley, and I couldn't tell if it was because he felt so badly about how Vernon and Mom had treated him, or if he just thought I needed to know the man that Elvis once considered a friend.

I had last seen my dad when I was about fifteen, before I went on the road with Elvis. I had gone with Billy, Ricky and some buddies to visit him, and it was a pleasant enough visit, although I couldn't say that I felt any real connection to him. To me he was Bill, the man who had brought me into this world and then left me. That's really all I knew of him.

He met Ricky and I at our hotel in Jacksonville. We had played a show in Macon, Georgia, then flew in that night and began partying at the hotel. The guys all looked happy, if not completely surprised, to see him.

"Well I'll be damned! Bill Stanley!" Lamar said, eagerly striding over to shake Bill's hand. "Boys, look who's here!"

Red greeted him warmly and introduced him to some of the other guys.

Finally, Bill spotted Ricky and me. I was leaning against the bar, hoping one more beer would calm the anxiety I was feeling. Bill walked over and held out his hand.

"Well, look at you – you're all grown up!" he said, sizing me up.

"Remind you of anybody you knew at that age?" Lamar asked, clapping Bill on the shoulder. "Looks just like you, Bill. Acts like you, too."

"Sorry to hear that," Bill joked.

I was surprised to see the ease of conversation and camaraderie between the men. I had always thought of Bill as a good-for-nothing

161

who everyone was glad to see gone. But what I was seeing before me was anything but that.

The next morning, Ricky and I went with Bill to the hospital where he worked and he proudly introduced us as his sons – and Elvis' bodyguards. His pride was so obvious, and his co-workers were clearly impressed that he was attending that night's Elvis Presley concert – with backstage passes, no less.

We took Bill and his wife, Lois, backstage with us before the concert. Bill was clearly excited by the experience, and he was happy when he heard that Elvis was about to arrive.

Elvis came in, flanked by his entourage, and Bill looked at him, stunned.

"Look what the cat drug in," he said, extending his hand to Elvis. "Man, you look terrible!"

I couldn't believe my ears. I knew that Ricky and I would probably be fired as soon as the show was over. *Nobody* talked to Elvis like that. I was literally shaking in my boots.

"Sgt. Stanley – good to see you too, sir," Elvis said, enthusiastically shaking Bill's hand. "How the hell are you?"

"I'm fine," Bill replied. "But you don't look so hot."

Ricky and I cringed again, exchanging a glance. Was Bill ever going to say the right thing? To our amazement, Elvis took every word at face value. He admitted to my father that he wasn't at his best.

"The road makes it tough sometimes, but I'll get back to fighting form real soon," Elvis promised him.

"You do that," Bill said. "I know from experience, it can catch up with you real fast."

I was shocked at the way Bill was able to talk to Elvis. I'd never seen anyone be that candid with him without paying a price for it. I was relieved when the show began, and I took my position at the side of the stage. I didn't notice where Bill and Lois disappeared to as I was now officially on duty and absorbed in what needed to be done that night.

Joe and I were talking as the show began, and Joe looked out over the crowd. A smile crossed his face and he put his hand on my arm, stopping our conversation in mid-sentence.

"David, look out there," he said, pointing.

At the front of the stage, the policemen hired to do security for that night's show had positioned themselves as instructed, ready for the crush of fans that inevitably came with Elvis' appearances. Locking arms with them and standing braced for the onslaught was Bill Stanley. Unbeknownst to me, years after a promise of becoming Elvis' bodyguard had been made, he was able to finally fulfill that destiny.

Bill stayed on with us for the remaining three shows in Florida, driving to meet us in each town that Elvis played in. I would later learn that it was one of the most powerful healing experiences of his life. He seemed proud of the fact that we were working together, and I was surprised at how relaxed he was around me. His first encounter with Vernon was surprisingly civil, given their history. I studied the man whom I called "Daddy" interacting with my father, and I began doubting everything that I had known to be true.

It had been so much easier to hate Bill for not being there, to despise him for his human frailties, than it was to comprehend the tragic complexities that had, in many ways, ruined his life. His losses had, indeed, been my gain, leading me to a life of privilege that most would only dream of. Now, as I met the man who had haunted my dreams, the myths I'd believed about him began unraveling.

Years of hating my father for the man I thought he was were melting away as I realized just what kind of man he actually was. I was stunned by what I was learning and, by the time we shook hands and said goodbye four days later, I felt a sad sort of anger for all the time that we had lost, even though I knew I wouldn't have met Elvis had it not turned out the way it did.

Close to the Edge

Most of the summer of 1975 was spent traveling. Elvis continued struggling with his weight, and during a June show in Memphis, he split the seat of his jumpsuit while bending down to kiss a fan. He made a joke about it, but it was obvious afterward that it bothered him immensely. He knew he was losing the battle with his weight, and given the battles that were beginning to break out with his own crew, he really didn't seem up to the fight.

Even when we didn't talk about it, everyone was aware that the drugs were taking a stronger hold on Elvis that anyone wanted to admit. The tension had remained so thick you could cut it with a knife ever since the blowup between Sonny, Red and Elvis in Vegas. In May, we sat in the hotel bar in Monroe, Louisiana after a show and, once again, the talk turned to Elvis' uneven performances and even less predictable behavior. Red and Sonny seemed convinced that the shit was about to hit the fan. Lamar tried to persuade them that they were over-reacting. We finished our beers and Sonny pointed his empty bottle toward me.

"Your turn to buy, David."

I sauntered over to pick up another round, and as I did, I noticed an attractive young woman at the end of the bar. She was dressed seductively, and the way she blew her cigarette smoke in my direction told me she was looking for a good time. I figured I may as well assess the situation and see if I could oblige her.

"Hey," I said, nodding at her. I turned just far enough in her direction for her to be able to see the "Crew" pass hanging around my neck.

"Hey yourself," she said with a smile. "Is that real?"

I smiled, fingering my crew badge.

"Sure it is. What're you drinking?"

"A flaming orgasm. Wanna share one with me?"

There really wasn't much point in trying to answer that question—verbally at least.

"Make it two," I told the bartender. "And can you send three beers to the table in the corner?"

We made it halfway through our drinks before we went back to my room, and things were moving along nicely when someone began pounding on the door.

"Police! Open up!" screamed a voice on the other side.

"What the hell ..." I jumped up from the bed and my sassy lady friend began frantically adjusting her clothes as I opened the door. I stood there, wearing nothing but a pair of jeans, staring at a large and angry police officer. Dick Grop, head of security for Elvis, stood at his side, looking none too happy either.

"Dick, what's the problem?"

Before Dick could open his mouth to speak, the officer filled me in.

"Mr. Stanley, it seems that we have a significant problem on our hands. The bartender tells us that you left the bar with a young girl."

He gave me the her name, which matched the name of the girl who'd been in my arms just moments earlier. I nodded.

"Yeah, I did. What's the problem?"

"David, her father is downstairs," Dick said quickly and urgently. Behind me, I could hear the girl begin swearing.

"Her father?"

"Mr. Stanley, did you touch her?" the officer wanted to know.

"What? What the fuck do you mean, did I touch her?"

The girl pushed past me, obviously embarrassed.

"Sorry David, gotta go. It's been fun!"

"Mr. Stanley, she's only seventeen..." He watched as she began to scurry down the hall.

"Don't leave," he advised me and then went after my underage date.

"What the hell were you thinking?" Dick demanded. "You just don't get it, do ya, David?"

"Dick, I didn't know. Honest! She was at the bar, she was drinking, she was smoking – how the hell was I s'posed to know she was jailbait?"

"Fuck! David, when the hell are you gonna start using your head? I mean the one on your shoulders, not the one in your pants?"

He was furious, and he hadn't calmed down much by the time we got to Elvis' suite. Dick gave Elvis a quick recap before Elvis started in on me.

"David, did you do it?" he wanted to know. It seemed so unfair! These guys were constantly sleeping with women – how in the hell did I end up being the one getting interrogated?

"No, Elvis, I swear. I didn't touch her. I was about to, then the cop and Dick knocked on the door."

"Boss, they wanna take him in," Dick added, a point which I felt he could have waited to bring up. "They sent the girl to the hospital to run some tests. If they come back positive..."

"Damn it, David! Do you understand that this is Louisiana? You don't fuck up like that here!"

"I didn't, Elvis, I swear! I didn't touch her!"

"What if someone else did? It doesn't have to be you that did her – coulda been somebody else and they're gonna pin it on you."

The reality of his statement hit me like a cold glass of water in the face. I realized that I could be in big trouble, maybe even too much trouble for Elvis to get me out of. I sat down, shaken, and within moments we heard a knock at the front of the suite. Dick went to answer it and returned with the cop who'd been at my door earlier. A second officer accompanied him.

"Excuse me, sir, but we're going to need to hold Mr. Stanley for the night. The girl's father is pressing charges," the cop said. I could feel my heart sinking to the floor. I didn't know how we were ever going to explain this one.

Elvis' voice was calm but firm as he answered.

"That won't be necessary, gentlemen," he assured them. "David tells me he's innocent, so there's no need to take him anywhere."

The officers looked at each other, nervous but certain of what they needed to do. "With all due respect, Mr. Presley, I have my orders..."

In a single, fluid motion, Elvis pulled his Federal Narcotics Officer badge from his bathrobe pocket and shoved it in the officer's face.

"...and I have mine," Elvis said. "From the President of the United States."

"You do realize that you could be exposing yourself to a charge of obstruction of justice..."

"I don't give a rat's ass about what you think," Elvis snapped. "Good night, gentlemen. Dick, show them out."

Dick began escorting them to the door, and the officer who'd come to my room earlier looked over his shoulder. "Mr. Stanley, I must advise you not to leave this hotel," he said as Dick herded them through the door. "We'll be in touch."

Elvis waited until the front door of the suite closed before he exploded.

"Goddamn it, David, if you're lying..."

"I'm telling you Elvis – I'm not. I swear."

"Dick, get the jet ready. I want him outta here tonight."

"But Elvis, he said..." I began lamely.

"Shut up, David. You're getting out of here."

I was on the plane within the next two hours and flew ahead to the next town, where Elvis was playing. By the time he arrived the following day, police had confirmed what I'd already told Elvis – I hadn't touched her. I was filled with relief and a sense of victory as he gave me the good news.

"See? I told you ..."

"Look David, you got lucky," he interrupted. "You gotta be careful out there. There's people who'd love to bring us down, and we can't afford that kinda headline. You got it?"

I nodded. I had learned a lesson, alright. It had scared me badly, shaken me to my core, but what scared me even more than the possible charges was the idea that Elvis had lost faith in me. I wanted him to believe in me the way that I believed in him. I didn't know if that would ever be possible, but I knew that I never wanted to see him look at me with a question in his eye ever again.

The summer wrapped up with an August engagement back at the Las Vegas Hilton. The schedule began on August eighteenth, but after three days, Elvis pulled the plug on it and went into the hospital yet again. He was having trouble breathing, and the three shows he had performed were far from stellar. He was weak and incoherent, and the entire time that he was onstage he looked as if he couldn't wait to leave.

This time, he stayed hospitalized until September fifth. I was disgusted by what I was seeing. I knew that the drugs were the problem. Without their intrusion into his life, Elvis was his usual vibrant, outgoing self. The more drugs he took, the more he faded. We were all his "yes" men as we had seen what happened when Red and Sonny tried to talk to him about his chemical excesses. So, angry

170

as we were about it, we all let it go on whether we agreed with it or not.

It hurt me to see what was happening to the guy I once knew. I was on duty in the hospital one night, studying him and trying to figure out who he was and what he was doing to himself. Elvis opened his eyes and looked at me, and when our eyes met it was as if he knew I no longer looked at him the same way I had 2 years ago. He knew that I knew he was doing this to himself.

"What are you thinking, David?" he asked me sincerely.

"You don't wanna know," I answered, unable to keep the edge out of my voice.

"What's that supposed to mean?"

"I really don't have anything to say to you right now."

Elvis looked at me for a moment. If there was one thing that Elvis treasured above all else, it was image. To know that his image was cracked or tarnished in anyone's eyes was something he just couldn't handle. He picked up the phone at his bedside and called Joe, asking him to come to the hospital.

We sat in silence, watching the television in Elvis' room, until Joe arrived. Elvis told me to wait outside while they talked, and when Joe emerged, he told me that Elvis wanted me to take the rest of the week off.

"What? How come?" I was incredulous.

"He doesn't want you in the room with him," Joe replied.

It hurt my feelings, but it also angered me. He wanted me out of there because he could see that I was judging him. I didn't approve of what he was doing to himself, and while I kept my mouth shut, my eyes said everything that my mouth wouldn't.

With the rest of the week off, Angie and I planned a trip back to Nashville to see her parents. We had a few days off, and it was always a nice drive, so my oldest brother, Billy and his wife, offered to go along.

We were in the car when Angie brought up the subject of my little black book.

"I found it," she said, her voice surprisingly calm. I thought maybe she was bluffing, trying to find out what really went on when we were on the road.

"What are you talking about?" I asked, feigning complete ignorance. Suddenly, she produced my address book and began reciting names and phone numbers. I could feel my heart skip a beat.

"Baby, you don't know what you're talking about. You don't even know what that is." I wasn't sure how I was going to talk my way out of this one, so I opted for the silent treatment. We pulled into a rest stop and as Billy and I used the bathroom, he warned me that the gig was up.

"You're busted, man," he warned me. "You're not talkin' your way outta this one."

"Shut up, Billy" I snapped back. "Everything's fine. You don't know what you're talkin' about."

We drove the rest of the trip in silence and faked our way through the evening with her parents. In our room that night, we resumed the conversation. I explained to her that, yes, those were all women from the road, but that none of them were mine. The guys all had girls on the road, and they couldn't very well keep the phone numbers in their own homes where their wives might find them, could they? So, I explained, I had become the keeper of the phone numbers.

She bought the story, but bought it with suspicions. Billy warned me that she was on to me and that I had better change my ways, but I knew I was incapable of that kind of change at that point in my life. I loved Angie, I just didn't know how to be faithful to her. The women I met on the road meant nothing; they were just warm bodies who helped me pass the time. This was the birthright of rock 'n' roll, and it had become my way of life.

Rocky Mountain High

We ended 1975 with a spectacular New Year's Eve concert at the Pontiac Silverdome in Pontiac, Michigan. The sold-out crowd of more than 62,000 people set a new record for the biggest audience to see a single artist in an indoor venue. Elvis loved Christmas time, and the holidays always seemed to bring out his best side, both at home and in the spotlight.

This year was different though. We spent the first two weeks of December in Las Vegas, where Elvis performed one show a night at the Hilton, and two on Saturdays to make up for the canceled shows in August and September. He again played to sold-out crowds, even though Vegas is notoriously slow during the holidays. By the time we returned to Memphis on December sixteenth, he was starting to show some wear from the gigs, and we all looked forward to wrapping up the holiday and taking a break.

The stage for the Pontiac show was a complicated three-tiered structure, much like a wedding cake. The speakers filled the first level. On the second level sat the orchestra and the band, and at the very top of this pyramid was the stage where Elvis performed. A tunnal was built to let him move from the dressing room to the bottom level of the stage undetected by fans. From there, he climbed a spiral staircase and then suddenly appeared atop the impressive musical mountain, much to the delight of the frenzied crowd.

Even before we had made it to the stage, the concert was plagued with problems. Before the show, someone had notified the police of a threat on Elvis' life, so security was extra tight in the sold-out indoor stadium. The stage was on the fifty-yard line, and after Elvis made it safely to the top of the stage, I took my place on the ground, eyes peeled for anything that seemed out of the ordinary.

It didn't take long for things to go wrong. Although this was a covered stadium and we were under a roof, it was bitterly cold and the sound system had trouble delivering Elvis' music to the crowd. The band was freezing, which made it hard to play their instruments, and with Elvis on a stage five feet above them, they lacked the interaction that was so vital to the live shows. Elvis had barely started the show when he began executing some of his signature karate moves on stage, and in doing so managed to rip the seam of his pants.

We had a second jumpsuit down below so Elvis slipped away while the band played, ran back down the stairs, and changed into the waiting outfit. What made the evening most memorable for me was the man who rushed the stage during the show. Since we already knew that someone had made a threat on Elvis, everyone was on high alert. When a fan came running across the field yelling something unintelligible, I wasted no time in confronting him and holding him while the police officers swarmed over us.

He was arrested and taken away. After the show, I relayed the story to Elvis, who at the time seemed only slightly bothered by the incident. It was another surreal day in a bizarre life that few people could understand, and even fewer people would ever experience. This was part of the price of celebrity, and I guess in many ways we accepted it just the same way as we accepted the limousines and private jets.

After the show, we flew back to Memphis on Elvis's new private jet, the "Lisa Marie". Each of us enjoyed our own personal New Year's celebration, knowing that the real celebration would come a couple of days later when we all headed to Vail, Colorado for a family vacation of sorts. In addition to myself, the extended "family" included Vernon, Ricky, Billy, Red and Sonny, Joe Esposito, Al Strada, and Dr. Nick and his son, Dean, who by then was working as one of Elvis' personal assistants. Those of us who were married took our wives along, and Elvis' companion was his long-time girlfriend, Linda Thompson. We stayed at a luxurious home that was right next to one owned by Gerald R. Ford, who at the time just happened to be the president of the United States.

Vail was a much-needed vacation for all of us, and coming off a hectic holiday season, it seemed as if everyone was ready to cut loose a little bit. The weeks in Las Vegas leading up to Christmas had been physically draining on Elvis, and he seemed relieved to have a new year ahead of him. In fact, Elvis was in particularly good spirits, and playing in the snow seemed to bring out his boyish side even more. Whatever tensions had built up during the year seemed to subside as we temporarily traded in our rock 'n' roll life for a few weeks of light-hearted family living in the mountains.

Not surprisingly, our schedules didn't change dramatically while we were in Colorado. Our days still began late and lasted long after the rest of the world had called it a night. We got an earlier start on the day than Elvis, and would spend the afternoons taking ski lessons. Once Elvis arose, we would venture to the slopes in the moonlight, playing on the snow-covered hills as if we owned them.

Elvis wasn't a skier, but he loved snowmobiles. The slope outside of our house was peppered with moguls, and we used the snowmobiles to pull a saucer-shaped sled to the top of the slope. The rider on the saucer would then shoot down the hill, hitting the succession of moguls, and getting the sensation similar to riding waves. The actual amount of time spent in contact with the snow was minimal, as each mogul would send the rider and sled flying through the air.

It was a dangerous game, but it was also a lot of fun, and we were constantly looking for ways to make it even more thrilling. We decided that since this worked so well on a sled, we might as well try it with a snowmobile. In retrospect, it's a miracle that nobody got killed. It seemed as if we were invincible, and even flying down a mountain slope on a snowmobile, barely touching the ground as we went, didn't faze us. Our lives had become all about flying high and going fast, and this was just one more way to do that.

One night Elvis decided he wanted to ride his snowmobile up to the peak of the mountain. It was a treacherous journey on thin, narrow paths, and any kind of a wrong maneuver would send the snowmobile and its driver over the edge of the mountain. Again, it didn't faze us. Just as we did in our daily lives, we blindly followed Elvis up to the top, and when we reached the summit, we paused to survey the mountain below us. It was a beautiful scene, and I felt like a god looking down upon his kingdom. The moonlight danced off the ice and snow, and the crisp night air was filled with a hushed kind of reverence broken only by the idling motors of our snowmobiles.

There was something magical about seeing the world this way, and we all stood there silently, captivated by the beauty below us. We stayed quiet in this rare moment of complete serenity when the roar of engines suddenly sliced the silence of the night. Looking behind us, we saw the bright lights of a pair of snowplows trudging up the hill toward us. Curious, we stood transfixed in the glare of their lights, waiting to see what was coming our way.

They were still several feet away from us when a voice came booming out of a bullhorn.

"Get off the snowmobiles!" the voice bellowed. "You are in a restricted area!"

We turned off our snowmobiles and looked at one another through our ski masks. Not sure what to expect, we dismounted and, as the snowplows pulled closer, we saw men jumping from their vehicles and running toward us. It was obvious that they were not pleased to find us there, and they intended to do something about it.

As the men came closer, I could see the security badges on their jackets and figured that we were probably on the verge of some kind of trouble. As soon as one of them began yelling, he confirmed that hunch for me.

"What the hell do you guys think you're doing up here?" he screamed. "You could start an avalanche!"

Elvis stepped forward, still wearing his ski mask.

"You don't have to get upset, sir," Elvis said, his voice thick with southern charm.

"Goddammit, you could get killed up here!" the man yelled back, and it occurred to me that for someone who was supposedly concerned about our well-being, he certainly wasn't being very nice. "You're all under arrest!"

Elvis pulled the ski mask from his head, which was basically the equivalent of a "get out of jail free" card.

"Oh my God, it's you! Hey, Elvis, pleased to meet you! How're you doing, man?"

The security guard's anger melted immediately, and he eagerly extended his hand in a warm greeting to the man he wanted to arrest just seconds earlier. He was completely enthralled that he was meeting the King of Rock 'n' Roll, and while he did eventually get around to admonishing us for being in a restricted area, he wasn't nearly as upset as he initially had been. We even received a nice escort back down the mountain. There was literally nothing that famous face couldn't get out of.

Our vacation started out relatively mild, but as we kept pushing the limits of safety, we had some close calls. None was more unsettling than the one that occurred one night while sledding down the moguls near our house. Dr. Nick and his son were just as willing as the rest of us to try something stupid, and as we watched, Dean Nichopoulos jumped on one of the metal saucers and made a flying leap toward the slope. It was a bad start, but once he became airborne, there was no way to stop. We watched as he careened off the side of a mogul, again becoming airborne as he clung to his saucer. There was nothing that we could do except hope that he could somehow correct his trajectory during one of his brief touchdowns on a mogul.

Dean's out-of-control ride continued down the hill, ending when he hit a fence pole. We all heard the sickening thud as his legs made contact with the pole, and we slid down the hill as fast as we could to get to his side.

Dean was yelling and writhing in pain by the time we got there, and Dr. Nick pushed us aside as he unzipped the leg of his son's ski suit. He pulled the suit back from Dean's leg and began touching the injured area, sending Dean into spasms as he screamed in agony.

"I think it's broken," Dr. Nick said. "We're gonna need to get him to a hospital."

"Let me see him," Elvis commanded, pushing Dr. Nick aside as he knelt over Dean's injured leg. He had a look of intense concentration on his face and he had taken on a commanding aura that was impressive and intimidating – even for Elvis.

"Hold on there, son," he said to Dean, trying to give him some sort of comfort. Elvis rubbed his hands together quickly, as if trying to start a fire in the palm of his hand. After several seconds, he moved his lips in a silent prayer, then placed his hands on Dean's leg. The younger Nichopoulos quit screaming and looked at Elvis, shocked. Elvis stood and backed away, and Dr. Nick scrambled back to his son's side. He pressed the flesh that had been excruciatingly tender just moments earlier. Dean looked at his father, shaking his head to let him know that it didn't hurt.

We all looked at one another, not sure what had just happened here. None of us said a word as Dr. Nick helped Dean to his feet.

"Are you okay? Can you walk?" he asked, his years of medical training refusing to let him believe what his eyes had just seen.

Dean nodded and cautiously tried a few steps. His face was just as surprised as the rest of ours; we had been through a lot with Elvis but this – this was something we couldn't explain and didn't dare try. We all made our way back to the house, the levity gone from our evening and now replaced with a kind of spooked, somber questioning as if we had just seen a ghost.

We reached the house and were still on the back porch, which faced the mountains, when the night seemed to grow even more supernatural. The back of the house provided a majestic view, with snow-capped slopes reaching toward the perfect, cloudless night sky. As we silently contemplated what had happened just moments earlier, a flash of light to the right of this picturesque scene cut through the darkness. It was a huge meteor, followed by a blue trail of light as it blazed through the atmosphere. As we watched, it disappeared behind one of the mountains, reappeared on the other side and then broke apart in a brilliant explosion of light.

You could have heard a pin drop. I felt hairs on my neck standing up and had a sense of being in the presence of something much greater than I'd ever known before.

"Wow, that's pretty cool," Elvis said, smiling as the flares of light disintegrated into the night. He seemed oblivious to our complete awe and confusion, and as we stood there in silent amazement, he retired to his room with Linda. For me, it was another of those unexplainable Elvis moments. He was such a curious blend of human weakness and supernatural strength, and I wondered what had happened to make him so completely different from anyone I had ever met before.

Bad Company

His fascination with anything involving law enforcement had led Elvis to strike up a friendship with members of the Denver Police Department when he performed a Colorado show in 1971. He became particularly fond of two detectives, Ron Pietrafeso and Capt. Jerry Kennedy. They, in turn, treated him like royalty. The men became good friends, and the men even let Elvis go with them on some of their drug busts.

They were as excited about their friendship with Elvis as Elvis was about being included in their police activities. On the spur of the moment one night, he went on a shopping spree and bought some $70,000 worth of cars, including a Lincoln Mark IV for Jerry Kennedy and a Cadillac Seville for Ron Pietrafeso. Word of his spending made the news, and I was in Elvis' room on the morning of January twentieth when Don Kinney, the host of the *Denver Today* morning television program, reported the story.

"Elvis, if you're watching," he joked, "I wouldn't mind getting a car, too."

Then Kinney went on to describe what kind of car he would like. Elvis looked at me. "You got that?" he asked.

I groaned, then nodded.

"Call the dealership."

Within moments, Elvis had me making arrangements for a new blue Cadillac Seville to be delivered to the station the following morning. We watched live on the broadcast the following night as the car dealership's manager presented the stunned host with the keys.

The threat on Elvis before the New Year's Eve show in Pontiac wasn't the first he'd ever received, but it seemed to bother him for quite some time afterward. I was on duty one night in Denver, spending a fairly quiet evening in Elvis' room. We had taken some Quaaludes together and were talking about a wide variety of subjects when he asked me what had happened to guy after the police took him away.

"He spent a couple a days in jail, I think," I answered.

"Do you remember his name?"

I nodded.

"Let's call him up."

"What?"

"Let's find his number and call him up."

After several dead-end attempts to find the man's phone number, Elvis called Jerry Kennedy, who was able to call him back a few minutes later with the man's correct phone number. I dialed the phone and made sure I had the right guy before telling him that I had someone who wanted to talk to him before Elvis snatched the phone out of my hand.

"This is Elvis Presley, you little chicken-shit son of a bitch," Elvis began. "I oughta get on my plane right now and come beat your ass!"

Even in my wasted state, I could tell that Elvis was pretty far gone himself. His colorful stream of expletives went on as he threatened to kill the guy – and his whole family. He continued his verbal assault until he finally felt vindicated and hung up the phone.

He was still beyond angry though. He ordered me to get the jet ready, saying we needed to fly to Detroit and "take care of that guy" that night. I let his tirade go on until he was exhausted, finally collapsing on the edge of his bed. It was just another day in the life of the court jester.

Most of our time in Colorado was spent footloose and fancy free, and often it felt as if we didn't have a care in the world. Even when we were technically on duty, we really were doing little more than playing, so the days passed quickly. Elvis spent time with his police friends, and after returning from a night out with them, Elvis called me into his room eager to share his latest adventure. A man who spent his life in the spotlight, adored by millions, was finding new energy from going undercover with his newfound friends.

"I went on a drug raid tonight," he told me excitedly, his face still flushed with excitement. He was wired, completely energized, and he paced the floor as he talked. I had already had a few hits off a joint and couldn't begin to match the kind of energy he exhibited as he walked around the room.

"Oh, yeah?" I replied. "What happened? Didja kill anybody?"

"Yes, I did," he replied, his face turning solemn but still excited.

"Really?"

"Yup, I did."

"Tell me about it," I said a bit doubtfully.

185

Elvis immediately launched into his tirade, recounting how they had gone up the mountain to a drug pickup point and found the cars waiting there. Elvis told his tale in vivid imagery, explaining how cold the night air had been and talking about how the light of the moon reflected off the snow.

"I was fine to hang back on the perimeter and watch," he told me. "But the narcos went down, the deal was made and then they pulled out their badges and showed 'em who they were."

"So I came around a corner, and there's a sniper sitting there. He was cockin' that rifle and had a silencer on it."

Elvis became more animated as he talked and I listened in silence, not sure where this bizarre story was going.

"I walked up behind him – he never even heard me – and I snapped his fuckin' neck."

He looked at me, waiting for a reaction. I wasn't sure what to make of it. I didn't believe for a second that this incident had actually occurred. It was the delusional fantasy of a man whose prescription drug fueled reality was more surreal than people's most vivid dreams would ever be. But I could tell that Elvis expected me to believe it, although I wasn't sure why. He appeared convinced that he'd actually committed this act of stunning bravery, and even went on to say that he had probably saved the lives of the half-dozen or so narcotics agents conducting the bust. An insane feat for someone with no law enforcement background or training, unless you count his so-called DEA badge of course.

But that was the way the world worked in our increasingly surreal lives. The lines between fantasy and reality blurred so frequently that it often became hard for us to tell where one ended and the other began, and even harder for Elvis himself. Part of it was, of course, a by-product of Elvis' heavy drug use, and as 1976 began, that habit was increasing at an alarming rate.

We were in the house one night, with everyone settled into bed, when I heard a loud thud in the hallway. Angie sat straight up in bed beside me.

"What was that?" she said, concerned and a little bit frightened by the sound.

"Wait here," I said, pulling on my pants. I didn't answer her question, but I had a pretty good idea as to what we had heard. Red, who was at the house that night, had heard the sound too, and he came running down the hallway from the opposite direction. We reached Elvis at about the same time. He lay slumped in the hallway, incoherent and unresponsive, so together we half-dragged, half-carried him into his room. We called Dr. Nick, who quickly appeared in Elvis' room, his ubiquitous black bag in hand. Red and I left Dr. Nick to do his job, and neither of us said anything as we walked down the hallway that led back to our rooms. We both knew that something had to change, but nobody knew how to go about making that change. I crawled back into bed with my wife, who was awake and awaiting my return.

"Is he okay?" she asked, truly concerned by what she had seen.

I shrugged my shoulders. "That's just Elvis."

"But he looked bad, David. Are you sure he's going to be okay?"

I nodded. He had to be okay. For his own sake and for the sake of everyone else – he just had to be. We knew that he was spiraling out of control, but most of the time, we were in an altered state ourselves and couldn't really judge the situation clearly. Still, even at our worst, we could see that something had to give. This was a speeding train headed for a nose dive straight off a cliff.

Two days later, it was my turn to be on duty when Elvis was wasted again. It was painful to watch him when he became so completely incoherent, when the man that I had admired since I was four years old would be swallowed up by a bloated, rambling, paranoid lunatic. Frustrated and tired, I began grabbing the bottles of pills that littered Elvis' bedside table. He watched me and then, in a single motion, drew the gun that he kept under his pillow and put it to my head.

"Put my goddamn medications down right now," he said firmly, suddenly aware of everything that was happening in the room.

"You gonna shoot me?" I demanded to know, even though I could feel my heart pounding in my chest.

"No," he answered. "But if you don't put 'em down..."

I threw the bottles back in a heap on his table and walked out of the room. For all the things I had been hired to protect Elvis from, it seemed the one thing I couldn't stop was the damage he was doing to himself. I was supposed to stop everyone else from killing him, but was forced to stand back and watch him kill himself. He had a serious problem, but he was also the boss. And in my twenty-year-old mind, that meant he probably could figure out a way to get out of this mess, regardless of how far in he got himself. My youth and inexperience prevented me from fully understanding that Elvis wasn't capable of coming out this death spiral alone--no one was.

We returned to Memphis a few days later, as Elvis was due to begin recording, and we were all pretty much done with our Colorado adventures. The time in Memphis was short-lived, as we soon got word that Eugene Kennedy, the younger brother of Elvis' Denver police pal Jerry Kennedy, had committed suicide. Elvis felt it was important to attend the funeral, and rather than take the entire entourage, we assembled a skeleton crew that consisted of Ricky, Al Strada and myself. Elvis made me go buy a suit for the occasion, and after some rather vocal objections to such an idea, I bought a black wool pinstriped number, throwing in an expensive black overcoat as a finishing touch.

The four of us flew out to Colorado and stayed at the Marriott Hotel, spending a couple of days there before the funeral. I knew that Elvis had other motivations for spending time in Denver. He had made a connection with a doctor there and was able to visit him to get his "medications" in addition to what Dr. Nick was administering.

He had a sense of urgency when he called me to his room the day before the funeral. I arrived to find him waiting in a full police captain's uniform, complete with the hat. I looked at him, eyes widened at the sight, not sure what this was about.

"Well, *that's* different," I commented.

"You know, later today, we're going to go down to the police department and they're going to swear me in as a captain," he proudly informed me. I could feel my eyebrows raise.

"Really..."

"And they're going to swear you in as a sergeant," he continued.

"Oka-ay," I said. Even after all these years and all that I'd seen, I didn't see this one coming.

"Um, yeah, cool, just let me know when."

As we talked, I had been fidgeting with my nose, and the movements weren't lost on Elvis.

"What's wrong with you? You got somethin' wrong with your nose?"

I explained that my sinuses had been giving me problems, and Elvis sprang into action.

"I got something for you," he assured me. He patted a chair by the table. "Sit over here."

He disappeared into his bedroom, returning with a vial of aqua-colored liquid and an assortment of supplies.

"What's that?"

"Sinus medication. I have the same problem," he explained. "I got this from the doctor here in Denver."

As I watched, he methodically tore two cotton balls in half and dipped them into the liquid. I had no idea what he was doing.

"Come here," he said, motioning for me to lean forward. As he tried to put the cotton inside my nose, I pulled back.

"Give it to me," I insisted. "I'll do it myself."

"Okay," he said, shrugging as he gingerly handed over the two soggy pieces of cotton. "Just put them in your nose."

I did as I was told, and as soon as I had placed them in my nostrils, Elvis reached over and squeezed my nose. I could feel every vein in my head opening wide as the pure pharmaceutical-grade cocaine hit my system. I was instantly on top of the world.

"Shit, Elvis, this stuff is great!" I exclaimed, feeling as if every cell in my body had just been given a high-voltage shock.

"I know!" he agreed, preparing a hit for himself. We were instantly sharing a spot on top of the world, feeling alive and invigorated. At that moment, I felt superhuman, and I could tell that Elvis felt the same way.

Our non-stop chatter was interrupted just a few minutes later by a phone call. I picked up the receiver.

"Capt. Kennedy is here for you," the voice on the other end of the phone informed me. Stunned, I told the receptionist that we'd be right down. I repeated the news to Elvis, who seemed completely unruffled by the revelation. He picked up the hat to his uniform and began walking toward the door. I couldn't believe this was happening. Not only were we both coked out of our minds, but I certainly wasn't dressed for the occasion.

"Elvis, look at me!"

He seemed to notice for the first time that I was wearing worn bell bottoms, a long-sleeve underwear shirt and boots.

"You'll be fine," he said, donning a pair of sunglasses. "Let's go."

I dutifully followed him out of the room, stopping at my own room along the way to grab a coat. The ride to the police station was excruciating. I could feel the coke-induced rush of blood making my heart pump furiously as the rest of me fought to maintain some sort of cool. Typically, a police station was not my destination of choice when I'd just filled my nose with cocaine. Only the bravado of Elvis Presley himself could pull this one off.

The honorary ceremonial swearing in that Elvis had referred to turned out to be much, much more. We were given a written test, then taken out to a firing range to pass the weapons portion of the exam. After that, we were photographed and fingerprinted, and by

191

that time, I was ready to come out of my skin. I knew that this was a gesture of kindness from Capt. Kennedy and his associates, but not everyone felt as warmly. The sergeant who assisted with my swearing in made certain that I knew his thoughts about having spent twenty years on the force before becoming a sergeant, only to watch some punk kid walk in and have the honor handed to him.

We managed to make it through the afternoon, and Elvis added a badge to the previously empty face of his captain's hat. He was unbelievably proud of his new uniform, and it was no surprise that he wore it to the funeral the next day.

I walked into his room on the day of the funeral, wearing my new pinstripe suit, overcoat and a pair of dark sunglasses. For all my bitching about having to buy a suit, I had to confess that I liked the way it looked. He had already been joined in his room by a couple of guys from the police force, and when I entered, they all stopped talking.

"Man, that looks like the baddest guy I ever seen," one of the officers told Elvis.

"That's the Head Hunter. That IS the baddest guy you've ever seen," Elvis assured him. The words bolstered my pride and stroked my ego. I knew that Elvis meant what he'd just said, and it reminded me of why I was there. I would follow him to the end of the earth if he asked me to, but a lot of times I couldn't tell you why. Love truly is blind sometimes. When I heard the fatherly pride in his voice, it resonated in a place deep inside of me, comforting me with a kind of peace that had been extremely rare in my life.

We sat near the back of the church and, as the funeral wore on, Elvis began to grow restless. It was a Catholic service, filled with the rituals of that religion and forty-five minutes into the ceremony,

Elvis decided that he'd had enough. As he rose to his feet I could feel myself cringing inside, wondering what he was up to now.

"Oh, hell, enough of this," Elvis said loudly. "Just go ahead and bury the son of a bitch!"

There was a moment of shocked silence as the entire congregation of mourners turned to look at the man who had just interrupted the funeral of their loved one. I held my breath, wishing the church floor would open and swallow me up. After a rather uncomfortable silence, someone burst out laughing. Another burst of laughter followed, and soon the entire church was laughing. All I could think was, "Thank God these guys are Irish." If there was any doubt that the Irish celebrate the passing of a life better than any other nationality, it was removed during that service.

Get Out of Dodge

Elvis had managed to keep his drug abuse under wraps up until that point, but during those days in Colorado, Ron Pietrafeso and Jerry Kennedy were beginning to get suspicious. They had known Elvis for five years, and they could see the dramatic changes in his behavior. It came to a head with them in March, when Elvis went back to Denver for a few days. It was a small group, and Elvis had finished doing some recording and he mostly wanted a break and to hang out with his cop buddies and blow off steam.

Ron Pietrafeso and Jerry Kennedy had been alerted by the police surgeon, Dr. Gerald Starkey, that Elvis had approached him after Eugene Kennedy's funeral, looking for some Diluadid. As a hard-core painkiller, it was normally given to cancer patients and the doctor found it curious that Elvis claimed he needed it for an ingrown toenail. (And yes, you read that right--an ingrown toenail.)

We had only been there for a day when Ron and Jerry came to the hotel. Ron spotted me and took me aside. He told me that they knew about Elvis' drug problem.

"The gig is up," he told me sternly. "We know why he's comin' here, and we know what he's doin' here. Take him home, or we're taking him down."

It was a serious warning, one given by a friend who also knew that he had a job to do. They knew what was going on with Elvis – it was impossible not to notice, especially for trained narcotics officers. And they couldn't very well have Elvis getting busted on their turf, particularly since Elvis had given gifts, such as cars and jewelry, to members of the police force.

Red took the lead and told Elvis we should probably get out of Denver. Nobody wanted to tell Elvis what was really going on as we didn't want to risk angering him or creating any kind of verbal confrontation. So we just slipped out of town as quietly as any entourage could, and never returned.

It was obvious to everyone in the entourage that Elvis' escalating drug use was taking a toll on him, but it had become such a part of our daily life that we didn't really think about its long-term consequences. Even if we had been able to stop him – which we couldn't – it would have been a temporary fix. Elvis' motto had, increasingly become "It's better to be unconscious than to be miserable", and he lived by those words more and more each day. The best that we could do was ride it out and see where this took us.

We continued muddling through our day-to-day life, with Elvis alternating between a great show one night, and a concert where he was barely intelligible the next. I could feel the tension rising in all of us; we never knew from one day to the next what kind of show he was going to have, or if he'd be able to go on stage at all.

Even with all the uncertainties in the life we were leading, it still didn't seem that it would ever end. Perhaps I just chose to live in a state of denial, but it was unfathomable to think of a time when Elvis wouldn't be there. My life, for almost as long as I could recall, had been with Elvis. No matter what happened, it seemed that he would always be okay. And he had to be for all our sakes.

The first time that I ever really questioned the mortality of my life on the road with Elvis came in the form of a phone call on July thirteenth, 1976. We were on a two-week break following a tour that included shows in North Carolina, Texas, and Oklahoma, and concluded with a performance at the Mid-South Coliseum in Memphis. I was home with Angie, and was lying on the couch with her in my arms and a joint in my hand when the phone rang.

"Let it ring," she implored as the phone invaded our private world.

"Nah, I gotta answer. Might be the Boss."

She gave me a look that I was seeing more and more frequently these days, a look that fell somewhere between annoyance and contempt. I picked up the receiver and was surprised to hear Red's voice on the other end.

"David, it's Red. Have you talked to Vernon?"

"No, man, what's up?"

"I wanted to let you know that me and Sonny – we just got fired"

Nothing that Red was saying seemed to sink in.

"Fired? Fired from what?" I asked, not sure what he was talking about.

"Vernon called and said he was lettin' us go."

"No way," I countered. "Red, don't mess with me like that, man!"

"David, I'm serious," he promised. "Vernon said they're cuttin' back expenses. Elvis didn't even have the guts to tell me himself!"

"That's crap, Red, and you know it. No way is Elvis lettin' you go!"

Red and Sonny had been Elvis' closest aides for as long as I could remember, and they'd covered his ass more times than I could count. Even though they got crossways with one another every now and then, they were family. I knew there had to be some sort of a mistake. Red and Sonny were more than just bodyguards, they were, in many ways, Elvis' conscience. When everything was spiraling out of control, they seemed to be able to talk some sense into him. I wondered what had happened this time.

"Twenty years with the guy, and all I get's a pink slip," Red continued. I didn't have the words to console him as my mind tried to comprehend what was happening.

"Red, man, I'm really sorry. I don't know what to say..."

"Well, I just thought you should know. Look out, David, 'cause you might be next."

I hung up the phone and his words sliced through me like an icy knife.

"What is it, David? You look like ..." Angie was watching me, concerned, aware that something big was going on. I didn't answer her, I just picked up the phone and dialed Vernon's number.

"Hey, Daddy, it's David," I said, trying to keep the panic from rising in my voice. "Red just called. Is it true?"

I could feel the hesitation on the other end of the line; Vernon clearly hadn't expected to hear from me so quickly.

"Yeah, David, we let him and Sonny go. It was just costin' too much money to keep everybody. We had to do it."

"But Daddy," I implored, not believing what I was hearing, "these guys are family..."

His voice grew cold and there was a sharp edge to his tone as he told me, "David, this has nothing to do with you. You and Ricky are fine. This is just business, and it's none of your concern."

Vernon hung up the phone and I stood there, the receiver in my hand, with the dead-end signal blaring in my ear.

"Baby, what is it?" Angie stood facing me, waiting to hear the entire story.

"Red and Sonny. They're both gone."

"Gone?"

"Fired. Just like that."

I re-lit the joint I had been smoking earlier and had a shot of scotch before I picked up the phone and called Ricky. He had already heard from Sonny and was experiencing the same sort of stunned disbelief that I was feeling.

"Jesus God, Ricky – what the hell is going on here?" I asked.

"Man, I don't know. I don't know about anything anymore. We just gotta see what happens next."

What happened next was that Elvis called me from Palm Springs, where he was staying, and informed me that he was sending a jet to pick up Ricky and me at the airport that night. We were to fly out to Palm Springs that night to meet with him and discuss the whole thing. Ricky and I spent the entire flight in futile speculation about what had happened – and what was about to happen. By the time we arrived at Elvis' house, we had played out every imaginable scenario in our heads.

"So you heard?" he said as we walked into his room. Ricky and I nodded.

"I heard, but why'd you let 'em go, Elvis?"

"I had to, David," he said sincerely. "They were costin' me too much money. They were costin' me lawsuits. I needed to cut some expenses."

In later years, I would come to the conclusion that the West boys' dismissal probably had less to do with money than it had to do with the fact that they opposed Elvis' ever-increasing appetite for drugs. I had seen both Red and Sonny lay into Elvis on more than one occasion, telling him to get rid of the drugs and get his shit together. I think Elvis just got tired of hearing it and, in the end, he decided that he needed his vices more than he needed Red and Sonny.

The Wheel in The Sky Keeps on Turning

The days that followed Red and Sonny's dismissal were unusually tense. A kind of somber melancholy seemed to hang in the air, with each of us saddened by the West boys' departure. We all knew that how we felt about Elvis firing Red and Sonny didn't make any difference, and nobody was feeling courageous enough to outright disagree with him at this point. This was Elvis' world, and he called the shots.

He had a small crew of people staying with him in Palm Springs, and when Ricky and I joined him there, we immediately noticed the tension in the air. Elvis was feeling defensive and paranoid. He explained that he was cutting back on expenses – way back – and might have to let go of some more people.

Individually, he called each of us into his room and asked our advice on who else should stay. Ricky and I were initially scared to death, knowing that with Mom and Vernon separated, Elvis wasn't obligated to keep us around. When he summoned me to his room, this time without Ricky, I was prepared for him to have changed his mind, and I was also prepared to plead our case.

"I really have to cut way back on people," he told me. "Who do you want me to keep?"

"I would hope you'd keep me," I replied immediately. This was no time to play it cool. Elvis smiled.

"Well, obviously, David, I'm doing that," he assured me. "Of course I'm keeping both you and Ricky. Who else?"

I began listing the people I wanted him to keep around – Joe Esposito, Charlie Hodge, Jerry Schilling, Lamar Fike, Dick Grob...as I continued through my list, I realized that I couldn't imagine any of those guys not being in my life. I thought about Lamar, who had been around me for as long as I could remember. These guys were my family, and it gave me an eerie feeling to think that someday they could be gone, just like Red and Sonny.

As it turned out, he didn't continue cutting back the way he had threatened. Ricky continued working as Elvis' personal assistant and I moved into a higher profile bodyguard job, working with Jerry, Dick, Ed Parker and Sam Thompson, the brother of Elvis' girlfriend, Linda. I still had my duties as a personal assistant, but I was finally reaching the peak of the job for which Elvis had been grooming me since I was sixteen.

Ricky and I stayed in Palm Springs for about two weeks as part of a skeleton crew that also included Al Strada. Elvis was doing a lot of drugs and his paranoia seemed to escalate daily. He had lost his conscience when he cut Red and Sonny out of the picture. It was as if he was afraid it would somehow slip back in one day, undetected, and begin to harass him the way Red and Sonny had. Elvis demanded to know who we talked to, what we talked about with one another, and grilled us constantly to look for inconsistencies in our story. It was like living with the head of the KGB during the height of the Cold War.

The escalating tension in the group led to a lot of pot being smoked. I already had a fairly steady habit, but our marijuana use definitely increased as the aftermath of Red and Sonny's firing took its toll. We frequently found ourselves bored out of our minds, sitting around the house in Palm Springs doing little more than waiting for something to happen. Elvis bought some motorcycles for us to ride, and one afternoon Al and I were off duty, so we took a couple of them out for a ride.

Elvis was awake and in good spirits when we returned, and he walked down the front steps as we pulled into the driveway. We were riding new Harley Sportsters, and they were both beautiful bikes.

"How'd they do?" he asked as we killed the engines and dismounted.

"God, Elvis, that's a cool bike!" I said. He smiled at my enthusiasm.

"I want you to have it, then," he answered. "You too, Al. That's your bike now."

"Elvis, you don't have to do that," I began, but waved his hand as if to silence me.

"I know I don't, David, but I want to."

"Cool! Thanks, Elvis!"

He smiled and left us there to admire our new possessions. Ricky joined us outside and the three of us decided to go smoke a joint in the garage. It had become a fairly common ritual for us, and we huddled in our little circle inside the garage as I pulled out a doobie and fired it up. I was taking a long pull on the joint when Ricky's and Al's eyes widened, then they both bolted out the side door. I turned around just in time to see Elvis walking into the garage through the main door.

It wasn't the first time he'd caught me smoking pot, but that didn't minimize the hurt and disappointment in his face. His eyes looked sad and frustrated as he stared in disbelief. I realized there was no point in trying to hide what he had already discovered, so I tried to be as nonchalant as possible.

"Hey, Elvis," I said, exhaling a mouth full of smoke. He shook his head.

"This is the thanks I get," he said, dejected. "I try to do something nice for you, and this is my thanks."

I didn't have the words to argue. He looked so disappointed, so saddened by his discovery that I just looked back at him. He stormed out of the garage and I knew that it wouldn't be long until he called me to his room. So I did what any reasonable nineteen-year-old would've done – I re-lit the joint.

Within moments, Ricky and Al reappeared.

"You chicken shits," I said. "Where the hell'd you go?"

Ricky smiled. He was famous for disappearing when trouble appeared. "Did he see me?"

"Yeah, he saw you," I lied. "What're you gonna do now?"

Ricky shrugged and reached for the joint in my hand.

"Uh-uh," I said, pulling it away. "This is mine. I'm going to probably be paying for it all night."

We returned to our rooms and it wasn't long until I received the expected summons over the intercom. Knowing it was time to take my medicine, I went to Elvis' room. He looked at me with hurt and disappointment as I walked in, and I felt a combination of compassion and indignance.

"Look, Elvis, I'm sorry," I began. "I do appreciate the Harley-Davidson and I appreciate everything you've done for me. But this is tough, Elvis. We're sittin' around the house all day, everyone's freaked out about Red and Sonny – you gotta cut me some slack, man!"

"David, you know how that marijuana is. You know how bad it is!"

They were tough words to take from a man who now spent more of his day unconscious than coherent, thanks to a cornicopia of narcotics. But in Elvis' mind, what he did was legal since his 'medications' were prescribed by a physician, and that made all the difference in the world.

"I know. I'm sorry. But look at the bright side..."

"I'm anxious to hear what that might be," he said.

"At least I wasn't a chicken shit who ran off. And at least when you called me back here, the first thing I said was that I was sorry. There's gotta be somethin' said for that!"

His eyes softened and he nodded. He reached over to the intercom and pressed down.

"Ricky, you little chicken-shit son of a bitch, get up here now!"

I was off the hook. I passed Ricky in the hallway as I left and grinned. Served him right for running out like that.

Elvis, of course, didn't stay mad at either of us for long. Ricky was impossible to stay mad at; he was a funny guy and Elvis found him extremely entertaining. In Elvis' polyester-clad world, Ricky and I brought a youthful spirit of adventure that Elvis admired, even as he was admonishing us for our behavior.

Elvis had the motorcycles he'd given Al and me shipped back to Memphis, and at the end of July we went back on tour. We stayed on the road until early August, then went back to Memphis for a few days. It had been a grueling tour of back-to-back shows, and it was obvious to everyone that Elvis' heart just wasn't in it anymore. At times his voice was so tired during the show that one of his backup singers would have to step up and take a more prominent role in his songs. It was disconcerting, to say the least, and what was happening off stage was even more alarming.

The man who had always been so full of life couldn't seem to muster enthusiasm for much of anything. I still caught glimpses of the man that I had grown up adoring, but these were fewer and farther between, and his happiness seemed to have disappeared. Once enthusiastic about everything he did, it now wasn't uncommon for him to return the greeting of, "Good morning, Elvis," with a cynical, "What's so good about it?" This wasn't the man I had come to love as my big brother, and I didn't like the guy that he was becoming. That made me saddest of all; I missed the man that he used to be, and I wondered what to make of the man that he was now.

I barely had time to re-connect with Angie before we were heading back to Palm Springs. She seemed to be getting used to this routine, and we barely discussed how little time we spent together. Things had been tense since she found my black book, but we seemed to have settled back into our regular routine. I was a faithful husband during my time at home, and a single man when I was out on the road. Angie didn't bother asking questions anymore, so I figured that either she believed me when I told her there weren't any other women, or she had come to accept it as part of the rock 'n' roll lifestyle.

Elvis wasn't bothering to get in shape for his upcoming tour, and the reviews on the last outing had been dismal. Elvis had battled with Colonel Parker over his lackluster performances, and sitting around the house in Palm Springs just seemed to exacerbate the anxiety and tension that was building in our camp. For me, that anxiety would often explode in anger. My already-hot temper was a powder keg with a fuse that now could be ignited by the smallest spark.

That led to plenty of skirmishes with some of the other guys, but mostly they were heated exchanges that died down quickly. Nobody wanted to mess with me when I was mad, and most of the time they did whatever it took to disarm my anger when it erupted. Everyone had their own way of dealing with what was going on around us, but it seemed that anger was all I knew. It was the only emotion I understood and could embrace fully. As it turned out, I would soon have plenty of chances to see just how far-reaching my anger could be.

As we went out on the road at the end of August, the 'sleep diet' doctor, Dr. Ghanem, replaced Dr. Nick for the tour. Elvis' heightening paranoia had him questioning everyone's motives, and he had called Dr. Nick in the middle of the night, swearing and accusing the doc of betraying him in some unknown fashion. We hoped that a new doctor would help, but instead, Elvis' shows were even worse. The review of our first show in San Antonio referred to his performance as "lackluster", which honestly was a compliment considering how abysmal the shows had become. The following night in Houston, he was so drugged that he was barely conscious for his show. He sort of stumbled and mumbled through his show, seemingly unaware of what he was supposed to be doing onstage or why he was even up there. It was a complete embarrassment for everyone, including the fans.

We watched in horror from the sides of the stage, and I realized that things weren't getting any better, they were in fact getting worse. His audience was still loyal, but I knew that would only go so far and they were reaching their breaking point. Elvis was falling apart at the seams, and I wasn't sure what that meant for the rest of us.

Joe called Dr. Nick and got him back on the road with us, hoping that a more consistent administration of medications would help the situation. It did improve things slightly, but nothing could resolve Elvis' bloated appearance and his increasingly downcast outlook on life. He was no longer drugged on occasion, it was now a daily occurrence. I saw flashes of the man I knew and loved in between long stretches of unconsciousness and semi-consciousness. It was both heartbreaking and frustrating. The only thing I knew to do was what I had learned on the road – I self-medicated with coke, pot, alcohol and women.

I was in Mobile, Alabama at the end of August, and I could barely hear the phone ringing through the haze of sleep. I tried shaking off the effects from the night before as Brenda, my flight attendant girlfriend and frequent companion on the road, fumbled for the phone.

"Hello?" I heard her say as she pulled the receiver to her ear. "Hello?"

"This is Brenda, who's this?"

She paused for a moment.

"Um, this isn't a very good time. Can you call back later?"

She hung up the phone and settled back into the bed beside me. I instinctively put my arm around her and pulled her closer, still half-asleep.

"Who the hell was that?" I mumbled, not really caring what the answer was.

"Your wife."

"Holy shit!" I sat straight up, instantly awake, nearly ejecting Brenda from the bed in the process. "What d'ya mean, my wife? What did you say?!"

"You heard me, I just – I..."

I paced the floor, suddenly wide awake, feeling panic race through my body.

"David, it's not that big a ..."

"Shut up!" I yelled at her. "That was my *wife*! Do you understand that? Oh, fuck! Dammit!"

I kicked the chair, sending it tumbling onto its side. Perfect, I thought. This is just what I need. More chaos in my life.

"You need to go," I told Brenda. She stared back at me, incredulous.

"What?!"

"I have to call Angie. I gotta work this out."

Brenda started angrily pulling on last night's clothes, now equally as upset as I was.

"Fine, David. Call your wife. But then don't bother calling me."

She stormed out and I looked at the phone. I lit a joint and took a couple of long hard tokes on it before I found the courage to dial. I knew that I was busted this time. There was no denying it. The best I could hope for was to lie my way out of it.

Angie was appropriately livid when she answered, but I managed to convince her that the woman she had talked to was only a friend.

"Baby, do you really think if I was seein' someone else that I'd let her answer my phone?" It sounded reasonable enough to me. I explained to Angie that several of us had partied the night before and that Brenda had gotten too drunk and had passed out in my room. Eventually, Angie reluctantly accepted my story. I knew that had been a close call, and didn't know how many more of those my marriage had left in it.

The tour lasted through the first week of September and, by the end of it, all of us were frustrated and exhausted. It seemed that nothing was going particularly well—at home or on the road. Things went from bad to worse when we started hearing rumblings about a new book supposedly being written by Red, Sonny and another fired bodyguard named Dave Hebler. Now, on top of everything else that was falling apart, Elvis was consumed by what he perceived as a complete betrayal by his former bodyguards. He would vacillate between angry rages and heart wrenching despair. First wondering how they could betray him in such a way, and then sobbing over the loss of his dear, one-time closest friends.

None of us had the courage to say what we all were thinking, because we feared that we would suffer the same fate as Red, Sonny and Dave. The fact of the matter was, Elvis had dropped them without warning, giving them a pink slip seemingly out of the blue. Worst of all, Elvis hadn't even delivered the news himself, but had arranged for Vernon to fire them. Of course they were angry at Elvis! Red had been with Elvis for over twenty years, and Sonny had been with him for sixteen. Nobody could blame them, but none of us wanted to tell Elvis that.

Happiness is a Warm Gun

Elvis was restless back in Memphis, so he took a skeleton crew out to LA, where we stayed at Linda Thompson's apartment. He bought a new Ferrari, but that seemed to be the highlight of the entire stay. He liked his new car, but it didn't bring him the kind of joy he used to find in cars and other toys.

Red and Sonny were out in Los Angeles, and Elvis was working overtime trying to put a stop to the book they were writing. They had enlisted a reporter named Steve Dunleavy to help write their story, and Elvis even had contacted a private detective named John O'Grady in an attempt to thwart them. O'Grady offered Red and Sonny some money on Elvis' behalf in exchange for them quashing the deal, but they declined, saying they had already signed the deal and now were obligated to finish it.

The crew spent long hours trading off shifts that involved nothing more than babysitting Elvis. These weren't the same kind of fun workdays I had known when I first came on board. We had to watch Elvis around the clock, since he was taking so many drugs that he spent more time completely obliterated than not. While he slept, someone had to watch him, because if he did happen to wake up, he would need help even walking to the bathroom. On more than one occasion he passed out in the bathroom and I found myself having to clean him up before physically dragging him back to his bed. I felt

213

more like a nursing home aide than a bodyguard. Although it was frightening at first, it soon became just another fact of our lives with Elvis. I was mad at him, but I also didn't know what to do about it. I was being paid to protect him and care for him, but the very orders I was made to enforce were sending him deeper into his downward spiral.

Part of our duties at this point included keeping up with his so-called medications and ensuring that he received them upon demand. We had "attack packs" – small yellow envelopes, each containing from six to eleven pills and a shot or three of Demoral. Elvis went through three attack packs a day, and they were numbered accordingly. He would receive his first one when he returned to his room at the end of the day before dinner. He now had his dinner served in his room, and whomever was watching him had to make sure that the drugs didn't kick in before he was done eating and put him to sleep, or else he risked choking to death, of which he had a couple of close calls.

Whomever was on duty with Elvis during mealtimes went through the sickening procedure of watching Elvis nod off mid-meal and begin choking on his food. The only solution was to reach inside his mouth and remove the food. When he woke up from his first attack pack, which lasted a few hours, he would ask for Attack Pack #2, which had the same quantity of drugs as the first attack pack, and would usually put him out for the rest of the night. In the morning, he would start the day with Attack Pack #3, which kept him sedated and numb from the outside world.

It was a maddening, mind numbingly dull routine. We convinced Elvis to let us fly in some girls from Las Vegas one night for a change of pace, and that at least broke up the monotony for an evening. But it couldn't take away the heaviness in the air.

One evening Elvis decided he needed more than the standard attack packs, so we took a Lear jet over to Vegas to see Dr. Ghanem. When we settled into the Hilton, Elvis demanded I get Ghanem on the phone

I dutifully called the number only to be informed that he was out of the country. I went back to Elvis to deliver the news.

"Dr. Ghanem's out of the country, Elvis," I told him. "They said he can't be reached."

"Find him," Elvis said, staring back at me with his eyes flashing with anger. I knew this wasn't something that was open for debate. I went back to the phone and began pulling every string and calling in every favor that I knew.

It took a couple of hours, but I was finally able to reach him on the private yacht he was on. He came to the phone and I explained that Elvis needed him – now.

"David, I can't do that," he snapped at me, exasperated. "I'm out of the country, I'm shuttin' him off 'til I get back."

"You can't do that! He needs you tonight, and I'm not about to go tell him that you aren't comin'!"

"I can't do it, David," he said before hanging up the phone. I made my way back to Elvis' room, knowing this was going to get ugly.

"Elvis, Ghanem doesn't have anything. He's not in the country and he's not comin' back tonight."

"You tell that son of a bitch to get his ass back here!" Elvis shouted at me.

"Elvis, I'm telling you. He's not coming. You're not getting anything from him tonight."

Elvis began swearing and pacing around the room. He grabbed a pair of .45 pistols from his cadre of weapons in the bedroom, jumped onto a table and began firing his guns into the ceiling.

"I'll buy a goddamn drugstore then!" he screamed, completely out of his mind in the throws of a drug induced tantrum. "I'm Elvis fuckin' Presley!"

Linda was sitting silently in the room watching the entire scenario unfold. Her eyes showed agony rather than fear, realizing she could not love him enough to save him. None of us could.

He emptied his guns into the ceiling then stormed out of the room. He found his Physician's Desk Reference and looked up some drugs, found the combination he needed and created his own cocktail. It accomplished what he was hoping for – it put him back in a state of numbed-out bliss, where he couldn't feel anything, especially his own pain.

The next evening, we flew back to LA and I put Elvis to bed. He took another handful of pills and passed out. Relieved, I went to my room and collapsed into bed.

I had only been asleep for an hour or so when Elvis burst through the doors and flipped on the light. I didn't know what was happening when he burst in, but as I opened my eyes, I could see that he was dressed in a black flight suit bearing the Drug Enforcement Agency emblem.

"Get up," he ordered. "C'mon, let's go!"

"What?" I asked blearily. "Where – what's goin' on?"

"Let's go kill those guys," he said.

"Who – what – Elvis, where are we going?"

216

"Red and Sonny. Let's go kill those sons of bitches."

I pulled my clothes on, not really sure what was happening, and hopped into the passenger's seat of his new Ferrari. He screamed out of the driveway and soon we were barreling down Santa Monica Boulevard, seemingly oblivious to stoplights and other cars. As he drove, Elvis swore that he'd kill Red and Sonny, swore that nobody crossed him and got away with it. I had seen him like this before and knew it was just the drugs talking – all I had to do was figure out how to get him to listen to me instead of the drugs. I decided to try a humorous approach.

"You know we're goin' to jail for a long time for this, right Boss?" I asked. "You think you're gonna be able to get us some girls when we're in there?"

"Shut up," he responded.

I kept thinking about the movie I had watched with Elvis called "The Valachi Papers." In the movie, the mobsters in prison all had silk robes, television sets and kept their businesses running from inside the prison walls. I wondered if we would be able to do the same.

"How bout beer? I like about a case a day. Y'think they got scotch? What about TV – they gonna let you watch Match Game in the clink?"

Now he wasn't answering me. He was staring straight ahead, focused on his mission. I realized that, even though it was the drugs talking, Elvis believed all of the voices in his head telling him he was invincible. It dawned on me just how serious this was, and I tried a different approach. It was truly the only thing I knew for certain could stop Elvis' rampage.

"I just wonder what Lisa Marie is gonna think," I threw out as a last attempt.

Elvis slammed on the brakes, sending the Ferrari spinning. Just like my life, everything around me was flying by too fast and completely out of control. When the car finally came to a stop on the side of the road, we sat for a moment in complete silence that was broken only by the sound of our labored breathing. I felt as if my heart was going to beat its way right out of my chest.

Elvis sighed heavily, then hit the dashboard with a leather-gloved hand.

"Damn it! I loved those guys!" he screamed in agony. "Why would they do this to me, David? Why?"

He began to sob and I was helpless to curb the tide of emotion overwhelming him. Nothing I could say was going to change anything. Elvis was a victim of his own actions on this one; he had dropped Red and Sonny without so much as a "thank-you," and after twenty years of undying loyalty, they deserved better.

"I dunno, Boss," I answered softly. "How 'bout we go back home?"

Elvis wheeled the car back onto the road and we returned to Linda's apartment at a much safer speed. His anger was gone for the moment, replaced by a deep, abiding sadness that was inconsolable. We all knew this book would be trouble. Elvis was about to be a disgraced rock star, and this book was about to show just how far the mighty had fallen. For someone like Elvis, to whom image was everything, that was a fate worse than death.

We were back in Palm Springs within a couple of days where we were met by some of the other guys and their wives, including Angie. Little had changed. The air was still thick with tension, as if all of us were waiting for the other shoe to drop. It made us all a little stir-crazy and I felt like I was always looking for a fight. It didn't take long to find it.

Several of us were at the house one day when Angie and I began arguing. It was one of those marital clashes that arise out of nothing and are so inconsequential that they're soon forgotten. I was doing a lot of coke, which looking back obviously wasn't a good idea, given the fact that we were basically stuck hanging out at Elvis' house. When I began arguing with Angie, she left the kitchen and walked into the adjacent living room, where Lamar and some of the other guys were sitting.

"Dammit Angie, I wanna talk to you," I yelled, following her.

Lamar stood up and stepped between us.

"She doesn't wanna talk to you right now, David," he said. "Why don't you just cool down."

I started to push past him and he extended a warning hand toward my chest.

"I mean it David. Let her be."

His words were meant to diffuse the situation, but they only made me angrier. I looked to the utility room on my right, where a dog training leash was lying on top of the washing machine. It was a thick, sturdy leash with a loop on the end, used for controlling attack dogs. It took just three steps to reach the leash, and I held it in front of me like a police baton.

"This is none of your business, Lamar. Get out of my way," I commanded him.

"David, goddammit, I said leave her alone!"

I pulled my arm back and put my weight into it as I struck him across the face.

"Son of a bitch!" he screamed as he dropped to his knees, grabbing his bleeding face in both hands.

"Jesus Christ, David, what're you doing?!" Ricky yelled at me as he raced from the living room to Lamar's side.

I stood there, my chest heaving, anger coursing through my veins, the leash poised to strike him again. The guys from the living room were on their feet, not wanting to get between Lamar and I, but not willing to let me do any further damage.

"You don't even want to get up," I warned him, throwing the leash back into the utility room. Nothing seemed to matter. The whole world was going to hell, and I was going with it. I went to find my wife, and she met me with a hug, holding me tight as if she never wanted to let me go.

It wasn't a particularly big house, so I was bound to run into Lamar fairly quickly.

"Elvis wants to see you," he told me later that day, his face red and swollen from my attack.

"You pussy," I spat back. "You had to run and tell the boss, didn't you?"

"I've had about enough of you, goddammit!" he yelled.

"Well then, come on. Let's take this outside," I offered.

He looked at me with contempt before stalking off. I shook my head and headed to Elvis' room to take my medicine.

Even though Elvis asked for my side of the story, I knew that I wasn't going to come out on the winning end this time. I was right.

Elvis was furious with me, as mad as I had ever seen him. I received a profanity-laced sermon about beating up the help that ended with him banishing me from his room.

"Get out of my sight. Just leave. I don't wanna see you," he commanded. "I don't care where you go, just get outta here."

I stormed out of the room, ready and willing to make good on his order. I didn't need to take this from him; in fact, I didn't need any of this. I packed a bag, called a cab and within a few hours I was on a plane to Washington, where I had a friend who worked for Concerts West. I spent a couple of weeks just hanging out with him, drinking and smoking pot to decompress. I felt like I was living in a pressure cooker and the lid was about to blow.

Meanwhile, Elvis had gone back on tour. They were about a week into a three-week tour when Elvis called me to come back on the road. I caught up with them after a show at the Notre Dame Athletic and Convention Center in South Bend, Indiana. I nonchalantly climbed aboard the chartered bus that would take us on the quick seventy-five mile trip to Kalamazoo, where we had a show the next night.

Elvis was already on the bus when I boarded, and he watched me, silently, as I made my way to an empty seat.

"Hey, Lamar," I said as I passed him.

"Sit down, damn it," he growled back. I knew then that things were back to normal and that everything would be okay. Like everything else that happened in our crazy little world, we wouldn't talk about it. I was back in my element, feeling relaxed from my time away and happy to be back on the road with the guys who I considered my family. About thirty minutes into the trip, Elvis made his way back to where I was sitting.

"Well, I didn't wanna talk to you because I wanted to talk to Lamar first and see how he feels about this," Elvis explained. "I just wanna make sure you guys got it all worked out. You guys are friends now, aren't ya?"

"As long as he doesn't mess with me, we'll be fine," I replied.

Elvis' quiet demeanor quickly turned to anger.

"Goddammit, David, that's what I'm talkin' about ..."

"I'm just kidding, Elvis! God! Mellow out, man!"

He smiled at me and shook my hand. I watched him make his way back to his seat and shook my head. I could already feel the tension coming back. I hated what was happening inside of me, hated what was happening to the guys I considered my family and, most of all, I hated what was happening to Elvis. I realized then that I really needed to smoke a joint, and the bus couldn't get to our hotel fast enough.

Fly Like an Eagle

We toured through the end of October, and in early November, Linda Thompson ended her four-year relationship with Elvis. It was upsetting for all of us. We liked Linda and knew that she was good for Elvis. She put up with a lot of crap that nobody else would have, and even though she didn't deserve it, we wished that she had stayed. With Linda gone, Elvis began dating some other girls, but I didn't even bother trying to keep up. Being in a relationship with Linda hadn't kept Elvis from seeing other women any more than my marriage vows had kept me faithful. To me, they just seemed like an endless parade of faceless, nameless girls that I'd been seeing for the past four years.

We stayed home for most of November, and Angie and I lived our life as we always had – riding Harleys, going to movies and not talking about what happened outside of our life together. She was kind and loving to me, but quieter than before. I couldn't tell if something was truly wrong or if we had just spent so much time apart that it was getting harder and harder to reconnect.

It was near the end of November when I decided to take my Harley out for a late-night ride. I had smoked a joint and thought a nice ride through the streets of Memphis would help me clear my head. I was cruising down Highway 51, and as I approached an intersection, I didn't notice the car that was speeding toward me.

He raced through the red light and turned into my lane. Suddenly I found myself staring down a car with no intention of stopping.

Whether it was the pot or the karate training, something else took over for me. I stood up, trying to get as much height as I could before the car hit me. I knew I'd rather fly through the air than underneath the car, and I didn't even feel the impact. I rolled over the car and into the street, and the next thing I heard was the squeal of tires and the sound of air brakes as the eighteen-wheeler barreling down on the scene tried to stop.

I could feel the tire of the truck resting against my side and marveled that I hadn't been crushed beneath it. Someone pulled me out from under the truck as a crowd gathered.

"Are you okay, man?" someone asked me. I felt like I was in a dream. I looked at my foot and saw blood pouring from my tennis shoe. I would later learn that my foot had caught on the car as I rolled over it, tearing it up rather impressively. I pulled the helmet from my head and watched as pieces of it fell apart in my hand. The only part left intact was the lining of the helmet, and I thanked my guardian angel for working overtime that night.

The paramedics put a quick, temporary bandage on my foot and rushed me to the hospital in an ambulance. I sat in the treatment room and couldn't believe my eyes when a nurse named Jo Beth Ferguson walked through the door.

Jo Beth and I had gone to the same high school, although she lasted a few more years more there than I did. She was a beautiful girl, and I'd had a tremendous crush on her back then. Her face showed surprise and recognition as she broke into a big smile. I suddenly felt like a little, insecure kid who just had been assigned a seat by the prettiest girl in class.

224

I was no longer freaked out about my foot; I was more concerned about looking cool.

"Hi, Jo Beth," I said, giving her my best smile. "David Stanley. I don't know if you remember me..."

"Yeah, didn't you drop out of school a few years ago?"

"I did. How are you?"

We flirted for a few minutes until she finally realized that she should probably attend to my foot. I spent a couple of hours there, getting my foot sewn back up and learning that I'd nearly lost a couple of toes that night. When they were done, they kept me in the hospital. I called Angie to tell her what had happened, and she called over to Graceland to let the guys know.

I hadn't been settled into my hospital bed long when Elvis called, his voice full of concern.

"I heard you went down," he said sympathetically.

"Yeah, I went down."

"You alright?"

"Yeah, but I don't think I'm going on tour with you this time." We were scheduled to leave the next day.

"I understand. But make sure you get all the medication you can. You don't want to end up without that," he advised.

"I will, Elvis," I promised.

"I mean it, David. And if you need anything ..."

I knew that wouldn't be a problem. Tish Hanley, one of Dr. Nick's nurses, had moved into a trailer home on the property of Graceland earlier in the year. Now, instead of going to a pharmacy to get his prescriptions filled, all we had to do was walk across the lawn and see Tish. Having enough drugs were the least of my worries. What concerned me was the idea of staying home while everyone else went on tour. I called a friend of mine.

"Make sure you get me some good reefer, 'cause it's gonna be a long two weeks," I told him.

I wouldn't have wanted to be Angie during that time; I was belligerent and angry, taking it out on everyone around me, but especially on her. Elvis called me a couple of times while they were on tour just to say they were all thinking about me, but that did little to ease my discomfort. I belonged on the road, and to think about them being out there without me made me pissed off at the world.

The tour ended with a stay in Las Vegas, which was a makeup tour for some shows cancelled earlier in the year. I later learned that it was probably good that I wasn't there as Elvis had trouble focusing and spent many of his shows offering rambling, often incoherent monologues. The reviews were terrible, and even the fans were finally starting to show their disapproval and lack of patience. When he left the stage on December twelfth, disappointed fans had no way of knowing that it was the last show he'd ever play in Las Vegas.

By the time the tour wrapped, I was starting to get around on crutches. My brother Billy had gotten me out of the house while everyone else was gone, most notably by scoring tickets to the KISS/AC-DC concert in Memphis. It helped raise my spirits tremendously, and by the time the guys were coming back home,

226

I was in a much better mood. Elvis called me the day they were returning and asked me to come to the airport in the limo to pick them up.

He walked out of the *Lisa Marie* with a new girl on his arm, and there he introduced me to Ginger Alden, his latest girlfriend. She was young, about the same age as me, and I found myself comparing her to Linda. I exchanged pleasantries with her, then Elvis reached in his front suit pocket and pulled out an envelope.

"What's this for?" I wanted to know.

"It's your tour bonus," he answered. Elvis was typically very generous at the end of a tour, giving bonuses to the crew.

"What's it for? I wasn't on the tour," I said, bewildered.

"Yes you were, David," he assured me with a smile. "You were with me every day."

I opened the envelope and saw $3,000 in cash inside. This was the guy that I had known, the generous man who wanted nothing more than for everyone to be happy. This was the guy I loved, and not because of the money. I loved him because of the heart inside him that made him so thoughtful. I wished he could stay, but I knew it would be just a matter of hours until he was drugged and unconscious again.

The holiday season was fairly routine. Ginger spent a lot of time around the house, getting to know the strange new world that accompanied her blossoming relationship with Elvis. I felt sorry for her in a lot of ways. Even though we were about the same age, I felt like a seasoned veteran in this world, and could see that she was often confused by the bizarre behavior of her new boyfriend. To us, it was commonplace, but to Ginger, who was expecting to date the man that millions idolized, it was a shock to realize the very large gap that existed between the man and the legend.

This had been a tough year on all of us, and we could feel its effects. I was with Elvis on Christmas Eve, and he and I sat alone on the back steps of Graceland. It was late, and everyone had left, and his little girl, Lisa Marie, had been tucked into bed. It was a quiet night, almost perfect in the way the stars lit the sky. Elvis became reflective and began talking about his earlier life, telling me stories about his mother that I had never heard before, and talking about his childhood. He spoke of coming from a meager existence and how he had never imagined he would come so far. His eyes had a sad, faraway look and I was struck by his wistfulness. There was a definite loneliness to him that no one could ever take away. He seemed saddened by the difficult year that we were completing, and despite the presence of a new girlfriend and a visit from his daughter, it seemed that he was constantly on the brink of utter hopelessness.

I didn't know what to make of it. I didn't know where the New Year would take us, if we would have a better year than 1976, or if this downward slide would continue. From the time he had found out that Red and Sonny were writing a book, Elvis' demeanor had slid even further into the abyss. I felt as if we had gone from a freefall into a nosedive. I just wasn't sure at what point he was going to pull it all back together, or if he even could.

The year ended with a New Year's Eve show at the Civic Center Arena in Pittsburgh. It was the perfect way to end the year and Elvis seemed to enjoy himself on stage and bantered with the audience. The reviews were positive, although they duly noted that Elvis was not the same man who had performed there just three years earlier.

When Elvis performed like he did in Pittsburgh, it gave us all the hope we so desperately wanted to cling to. We saw glimpses of his greatness, and wished we could capture that moment and hold onto it forever. But we knew we couldn't. Time wasn't standing still or turning back for anybody, not even Elvis Presley.

Stairway to Heaven

We rang in 1977 rather uneventfully in Memphis, while secretly hoping for a much better year than the one that had just concluded. The New Year's Eve concert in Pittsburgh seemed to bode well for the future and I couldn't have been the only one hoping that Elvis had turned the corner and would soon return to his previous greatness. We really couldn't afford to keep having the kind of shows that Elvis had put on during 1976. We were cautiously optimistic, but also realistic about the situation at hand.

A sparse crew – me, Al Strada and Ricky – flew to Palm Springs for Elvis' forty-second birthday in January. As usual, everyone wrestled with what to give him as a birthday gift. What do you buy the man whose pocketbook knows no limits, the man who can buy whatever he wants with a snap of his fingers? After much thought, I finally settled on a book about the John F. Kennedy assassination. Elvis was fascinated with the circumstances surrounding Kennedy's death, and even claimed to have a top-secret copy of the FBI report revealing who really killed JFK, though I secretly thought that was just another one of his delusions.

The rest of the guys would show up later to help celebrate, but since I was on duty on his birthday, I was there when he first got up. I offered a "Happy Birthday" instead of my customary "Good Morning," then took advantage of the time alone to present him with the book. He was extremely happy with his gift, perhaps because he knew that a lot of thought had gone into getting something that he was truly interested in.

As Elvis' day began that January eighth, I ate breakfast with him and we sat alone in his living room, talking about the year that lay ahead of us. What struck me most that day was the sadness that filled the room. He knew that he wasn't the sex symbol that he once had been, he knew his ability to care for himself physically was gone, and that he no longer had the commitment to his career that had driven him to the top. In essence, he wasn't Elvis Presley anymore. The newspaper reviews had not been kind to him and, even if they had been, he knew his performances were not what they used to be. At forty-two, he was a fading star, and fading fast. For someone who had lived in the spotlight for the past twenty years, it was impossible to fathom a life outside of its glare.

Elvis' face showed the weight of the year that had just ended. Even though he claimed that his budding relationship with Ginger had lit a new fire in his heart, his eyes belied that claim. As we talked that day over breakfast, I noticed just how exhausted he was. It wasn't the kind of exhaustion that can be resolved by rest, he was exhausted by all that he kept inside of him and all that he was trying to live up to.

In the few weeks since Christmas, I had noticed that Elvis was trying to be nicer to those around him, and I thought that maybe he was turning over a new leaf. He had a notoriously vile temper, and he seemed to be trying harder to reign it in and be more understanding of what others were going through. I wasn't sure what was going on inside of him, because he was never one to open up and communicate. I knew that he and his friend, Larry Geller, were spending a lot of time together talking, and thought maybe that had something to do with some of the changes I had seen in him.

He was reading even more than usual, mostly about spiritual journeys and awakenings. Elvis was particularly interested in the Shroud of Turin, and read everything about it that he could get his hands on. I read all these signs as his attempt to get himself together, and I hoped with everything inside of me that he would be able to pull it off.

We were back in Memphis by the end of the month, but we already had started planning a trip to Hawaii in March. It would be the perfect vacation, a chance for everyone to relax, and perhaps it would dissolve the gray cloud that seemed to follow us ever since Red and Sonny's departure. I knew that some time away with Angie couldn't hurt-- we were drifting farther and farther apart. Ever since the phone incident with Brenda, things had been different. I thought she believed my story, but I also knew that she wasn't nearly as warm toward me as she used to be. Some time in paradise could be just the thing to put us back on track.

Elvis proposed to Ginger on January twenty-sixth, and no one was more surprised than I was. In many ways, I felt sorry for Ginger. She had come into our world expecting to be courted by the world's greatest sex symbol. What she got, at that point in his life, was a man who was more interested in escaping life than living it. I would find myself defending her to Elvis, whose paranoia was making him more and more controlling. Ginger wanted to leave Graceland at night and go see her family, and Elvis wanted her to stay there.

"Come on, Elvis, she just wants to go home and be with her family – can you blame her?" I asked on more than one occasion as an angry, bewildered King tried to understand why she wouldn't want to spend all her time at his side. Her quest for freedom made him more controlling and paranoid than ever, complaining that she didn't realize he needed her, and I wondered silently why he thought she would want to sit around and talk to her boyfriend's stepbrother while her boyfriend slipped into his nightly coma. At one point, Elvis even had one of the guys slash the tires on Ginger's car so she would be forced to stay in for the evening. He had completely gone off the rails.

I couldn't understand their relationship at all. I didn't know if he just needed to be with somebody and she was willing to comply for the cache of saying she was engaged to Elvis Presley. I didn't see the kind of spark and happiness that I had seen between Elvis and his other girlfriends. It was as if he had made up his mind to marry Ginger, and he wasn't going to let anything stand in his way. Of course, I wasn't one to be analyzing relationships – I had plenty to deal with on my own home turf. I was too wrapped up in Elvis' world to realize how badly things were falling apart in my own. Because my entire life revolved around making sure that all of his needs were met, I failed to meet the needs of my wife, or even of myself. Inside, I knew that things were wrong, but I didn't have a single clue as to how I could fix them. Nothing in my life had taught me how to sit down and care for anyone other than Elvis, and now the world was spinning too fast for me to try and reassess my decisions.

We were back on tour in February for about ten days, performing in southern states from Florida to Georgia. The shows were mostly uneventful, and in March we headed to Hawaii for our much-anticipated two-week vacation. About thirty of us made the trip. For Angie and me, it was both our much-delayed honeymoon, and a last-ditch effort for me to save my failing marriage.

234

Elvis rented a house on the beach where he stayed with Ginger and a few other people, while most of us stayed at the Hilton Rainbow tower. It was the most relaxed I had seen Elvis in a long time, and it was the most relaxed that I had been in a long time as well.

Angie and I took the time to reconnect when I wasn't hanging with Elvis. With an interest in photography, I took roll after roll of film, mostly pictures of my wife and the gorgeous Hawaiian landscapes. So much tension had built up in our marriage, but the soothing environment of the island eased the silent hostility that had hung between us for so long. We spent hours alone together, and I was reminded time and time again of why I had fallen in love with this beautiful girl.

Even our time with the rest of the crew was more fun than anything we had experienced in the past several months. We played football, hung out in the sun, and laughed more than we had in quite some time. Everything was going well – Elvis was in good spirits and his energy seemed to be returning – when I got the call that he needed to go to a doctor.

I knew our fun-filled vacation had come to an end. It was a common practice of Elvis'. We would be having a good time and he'd be full of life, not depending as heavily on his medication, when suddenly out of nowhere he would decide he needed to see a doctor. So off we'd go, either to a dentist for a "tooth problem" or a foot doctor for an old injury that happened when he'd been thrown from a horse years earlier. He used either of those "afflictions" as an excuse to get pain medicine, and once he loaded up on drugs, all bets were off. This time around we went to a dentist, and Elvis got the pain medication he needed to help him escape from the real world that the rest of us had been enjoying so thoroughly.

Four days before we were scheduled to go home, the Hawaiian vacation came screeching to a halt. As much fun as we were having, he just couldn't stand having to be awake and present in his own life. I was mad at him – again – but knew it was pointless.

We launched our second tour of the year at the end of the month, but it was obvious to everyone that Elvis was an empty shell of his former self. If the critics were harsh, the fans were forgiving, and the screaming throngs seemed in sharp contrast to the scathing reviews. Behind the scenes, things were worse than ever. In Norman, Oklahoma, Elvis was so drugged that he passed out while eating. It wasn't that uncommon an occurrence, but this time around he still had food in his mouth when he passed out. I realized that he was choking to death and had to physically pull the food out of his throat myself.

It was a pathetic and tragic sight. I looked at him, reclining obliviously on his bed, his bloated face a seeming parody of the handsome man I had grown up with. I didn't know whether to cuss him out or break down and cry. Not that he would have known or cared either way.

He was over an hour late getting to the stage two days later in Austin, and while we announced that the delay was due to technical problems, the fact that he was slurring his words on stage added plenty of skepticism to that flimsy excuse. It was increasingly difficult to get him on stage, and we were growing more anxious and frustrated with each passing day. Many of his shows ran less than an hour long, and his lyrics and between-song banter were often unintelligible. It was painful to watch and we felt helpless. There was no real solution to this problem. Cutting him off from his supply was a short term fix – if we didn't give it to him, someone else would. We knew the drugs were only the symptoms of the problem, but as long as Dr. Nick and Dr. Ghanem were only a phone call away, those symptoms would persist.

We were in Baton Rouge, Louisiana, when the bottom finally fell out. I went up to his hotel room shortly before showtime, and found some of the guys hanging out watching television. Every last one of us was bone tired. I knew we all had aged a decade from the first ten days of this tour. Unlike the early days, when Elvis would be up for several hours before doing a show, he was now getting up barely an hour before he was scheduled to go on stage. If we couldn't rouse him, we would simply keep at it until we got him out of bed, then stuff him into his jumpsuit and get him to the stage as quickly as possible.

"He up yet?" I asked as I walked into the suite. Vernon shook his head no.

I sighed. I was so tired of each day being a struggle. I knocked on Elvis' bedroom door and walked in without waiting for an answer.

"Hey Boss?" I was disappointed – but not surprised – to find him still in bed.

"Boss? You gotta get up, man. You got a show to do."

"David, I can't. Get the doc in here."

"What d'ya mean, you can't? We've got a packed house out there!"

"David, damn it, just get the doc!" he snapped at me.

I could tell he was stoned. Angrily, I turned on my heel and stalked out of the room, slamming the door behind me. The guys looked up as the door slammed.

"What's wrong?" Vernon asked.

I didn't answer, I just glared at him and picked up the phone. I dialed Dr. Nick's room and told him to get to Elvis' room – now. Just then, Lamar came into the suite.

"What's going on? Where's Elvis?"

"He won't get up," I fumed.

"What? He has to – J.D. just started his set."

"He's out of it, man," I continued. "He can't get up."

Dr. Nick entered with his black bag in hand and pushed past us, heading straight for Elvis' bedroom. Lamar watched in angry silence. As the door closed behind the doc, Lamar erupted.

"Son of a bitch! Not again! He's on in forty minutes."

"It's alright," Vernon said, his voice tired and heavy. "Doc'll fix him right up."

"Well, he better," Lamar continued. "We cancel another show and there'll be a fuckin' riot on our hands."

I walked into Elvis' bedroom and found Dr. Nick sitting on the side of the bed, taking Elvis' pulse. His face was etched with concern and he shook his head as I looked at him. He motioned for me to join him outside and Elvis, barely coherent, didn't even acknowledge that I had come back into the room. He closed his eyes and I marveled at how bad he looked. His skin was pale and pasty; his breathing was shallow and his puffy face looked like a caricature.

"You're killin' us, man," I fumed aloud. Elvis opened his eyes and glared at me. I glared back, then silently followed the doc to the living room.

"How's he doin'?" Vernon asked.

The doc shook his head.

"He's not goin' on," Dr. Nick said. "His pulse is real slow. If I give him something now, he could go into cardiac arrest."

Joe looked at Vernon, unsure of what to do.

"Vernon, you know if we cancel now, we're getting sued."

We all looked at Dr. Nick.

"You go out there and tell 'em that Elvis is sick. Then you get him back to Memphis and check him into the hospital for exhaustion and fatigue. That oughtta keep 'em off your back," Dr. Nick suggested.

We all stared at one another in disbelief. This story just kept getting worse by the minute. It was bad enough to have him forgetting the words to his songs and walking off stage early, but now he couldn't even make it to the stage.

"Damn it, here we go again," Lamar said. "David, I need you to go out there and tell the crowd."

"What? Why me?"

"Just do it."

I took a limo on the short ride from the hotel to the Louisiana State University auditorium, and waited while J.D. Sumner and the Stamps finished their warm-up act. When I walked onto the stage, the crowd immediately knew something was up. I had faced crowds before, but I had never had to give them news like this. It was one of the very few times in my bodyguard career that I felt truly nervous.

I tried to explain to the eager crowd that Elvis was ill and would not be appearing that night. As soon as the words were out of my mouth, pandemonium broke loose. The crowd began to boo and yell, and many of them rushed toward the stage. Tonight, instead of being the protector, I found myself in the role of having to be protected. It took several policemen shielding me and shoving through the crowd outside the back door of the auditorium to get me safely to the car. At Joe's direction, I had promised the crowd that Elvis would reschedule his concert and that we'd be back to honor every ticket holder who was there that night. It didn't matter. This was an angry mob, and I probably could have promised them a personal audience with Elvis himself and that still wouldn't have calmed them down.

By the time I got back to the hotel, Vernon and Dr. Nick had made arrangements for us to fly back to Memphis and check Elvis into Baptist Memorial Hospital. We helped Elvis onto the plane, leaving him in the bedroom with Dr. Nick to watch over him as we made the flight home. I sat beside Lamar and wondered out loud what was happening.

"I wish I had an answer for ya, David," he said. "The things he's doing now – it's like he's regressing. Tryin' to go back in time."

I was puzzled by his words and asked what he meant, and he began pointing out things that my young mind had not yet connected. He was no longer concerned about what he ate, although he often made disparaging remarks about his own weight, and he didn't seem concerned enough to do something about it. Instead, he was eating foods that Lamar hadn't seen him eat in twenty years, food he used to enjoy when his mother was alive. As a young man, he had gone to the fairgrounds frequently, and now he was beginning to do that again. Was it an aging star trying to rekindle the excitement of his youth, or a dying man paying last visits to the things he had once held dear? We didn't have the answer for that. Nobody had the answer except Elvis, and he was too incoherent to say either way.

I'm Losing You

I was angry about everything that was happening; angry that the tour had been cancelled, angry that Elvis was spiraling downhill, angry that I was helpless to stop him. We checked him into the hospital, and I caught a ride home, surprising Angie as I returned early from the tour. Her happiness at seeing me quickly faded as my foul mood worsened. Instead of being happy to be home with my wife, I was in a rage over Elvis canceling the tour. I popped a handful of Valiums before pouring myself a tall glass of scotch. As I drank, I paced the apartment, swearing and yelling about how Elvis was fucking everything up. Angie let me rant, saying little, knowing that whatever she did say was probably in vain. Eventually, the Valium kicked in and I finally went to bed.

Sleep did nothing to take the edge off my anger. It was as if it had only intensified overnight. When I woke up the next morning, Angie asked me if I felt better. That was all it took to set me off.

I looked at my suitcase sitting beside the door and yanked it open. There, I found the guns that I normally wore when I was on duty. I pulled them from my suitcase and began firing them into the ceiling. Then I picked up a baseball bat, shattering glass into the mirror and the china cabinet before turning my rage upon the fish tank. Water and fish gushed to the floor as the glass crumbled.

"Fuck it," I screamed. "Just fuck everything."

I grabbed my car keys and walked out the door. It didn't take long to lose control of my car and wrap it around a tree. Fortunately, I did that in front of the apartment complex where Ricky lived, and he was one of the first to arrive on the scene.

When I regained consciousness later that day, the first thing I saw was my mom sitting in a chair by my hospital bed. I looked at the IV in my arm and tried to make sense of what I was seeing.

"David? Can you hear me?" my mom asked, and I could see that her eyes were filled with concern. "Son?"

I looked around, trying to assimilate everything in my brain. I moved my head and it felt heavy, like it was made of lead, but it also burned as if someone were sticking it with hot pokers.

"Ouch!" I reacted. "What happened?"

"You had an accident, son. But the doctor says you'll be fine, so don't worry."

"My car – where's my car?"

She looked at me and shook her head.

"That's not important right now. You're going to be okay – that's what's important. Angie's on her way here to see you."

She appeared at the door, her face tired and with a tight smile across it. My mom sensed the tension in the air and excused herself.

"You take care, son," she said. "I'll leave you two."

Angie walked over, looking at me with the eyes I had once melted into. Now those eyes looked sad and distant, and I wondered vaguely what she was thinking.

"I heard you roughed up a tree pretty good," she said, giving me a smile that failed to reach her eyes.

"Car's fixable. Are we?"

I wanted her to say yes, to tell me that all was forgiven and everything would be fine. Instead, she gave me a long, silent gaze.

"Angie, you gotta understand. He was there for me when nobody else was. I gotta be there for him."

"Who's going to be there for me, David?"

I couldn't answer.

"That's what I thought."

She stood to leave and I tried reaching out to stop her. A pain shot through my head and I quickly sank back down into my pillow.

"Angie, baby, come on – is there anything I can do to fix it?" I said weakly.

She stopped, turning to look at me.

"You can try, David, but I don't know if we can fix this. I love you, but I need you in my life more. I need more from you."

"I'll try, I swear it," I promised her, and I meant it. I didn't want to lose her.

She walked back to my bed, bent down and gently kissed my forehead.

"Okay," she whispered. "Let's try again."

Ironcially, I was just two doors down from Elvis, and that night he came to my room.

"What're you doing here?" he asked me.

"Same thing you are," I said sarcastically. "Drying out."

"You okay?" he asked me, and I wasn't sure how to answer. I nodded, telling him I should be out any day now, so I'd be back to work as soon as I could. He asked if they were giving me enough medication to help with the pain.

"Yeah," I answered. "It still hurts some, but it's better."

He patted me on the shoulder and smiled.

"You know, David, sometimes it's better just to be unconscious than to be miserable."

Those were words that would haunt me for years to come. For the first time, I knew that he truly did not want to be conscious in this world any longer. He lived for those times when he slipped out of the real world and into a comfortable state of nothingness. It saddened and angered me, but I also knew that there was nothing that I – or anyone else – could do to make him see the world any differently.

We spent a couple of weeks healing, and were back on the road by mid-April for a brief tour. The press was picking up on Elvis' deteriorating condition, and even questionable publications like *The Star* and *National Enquirer* were running touched-up photos that looked even worse than anything I had seen, even on Elvis' worst days. We finished the tour and made it back to Memphis, just grateful to have made it through another tour without any shows being cancelled.

We had a couple of weeks off until we went back on the road, so I spent time either on duty with Elvis or trying to prove to Angie that we could make this work. It would have been easier if, like

246

many couples, we had just quit liking each other. But the problem was, we always had a good time together. Neither of us were ready to walk away, but we both knew that the burden of keeping the relationship together was becoming heavier and heavier, especially for Angie.

My extramarital activities had never been hampered by Angie's suspicions. It seemed that I was always able to lie my way out of any situation that appeared questionable to my wife. I was still carrying on my affair with Brenda, and since she was frequently a flight attendant on the plane that the band traveled on, it was impossible not to see her. This was a temptation too great to resist. When we weren't touring, I continued trying to make things work with Angie, but my wedding vows were paused when I climbed aboard the *Lisa Marie*.

Even though Angie was still hanging in there with me, I noticed that she had begun to keep a much closer watch on my activities. When we went back on the road at the end of May for a two-week tour, I invited her to join us. It would be fun for us to be on the road together again, and I knew it would keep me out of trouble. She jumped at the chance.

Angie couldn't get out of work for the first night of the tour, so we agreed to meet at the bar of the hotel the band was staying at in Louisville, Kentucky the next night. I was sitting in the hotel bar drinking a glass of scotch when she walked in with her suitcases. She was always a striking sight to behold, with her long legs and long dark hair only briefly offering a distraction from her beautiful face. She saw me sitting at the bar and smiled at me as she walked over.

"Hey," I said, smiling at her as I rose from my stool and began moving toward her.

"Hey yourself," she returned, putting her suitcases down. As we began maneuvering around the baggage at our feet, some of the crew from the tour made a noisy entrance. Brenda immediately spotted me talking to a tall, raven haired beauty and took matters into her own hands. Walking directly over to me and without blinking an eye, she wrapped her arms around me and stuck her tongue straight down my throat.

"This is going to be our best tour yet!" she exclaimed as she pulled away.

I was horrified as I immediately looked over at my wife. All that remained where Angie had been standing were her suitcases.

"Oh, shit," I said, pushing Brenda away and running for the door. Angie was already climbing into a cab by the time I made it outside.

"Angie! Wait – come here," I yelled hopelessly as the cab pulled away. She didn't look back.

"Damn it!" I screamed, not believing this was happening. I knew that this would be the last straw for her. There was no way that I was talking or lying my way out of this mess. I pulled the wedding ring from my finger and launched it into the air, watching as it broke the surface of the pond surrounding the hotel fountain.

"Shit! Shit! Shit!" I wanted to break something with my bare hands. I wanted something else to be as broken as my marriage.

When I walked back into the hotel bar, Brenda was perched on the stool I had been sitting on just moments earlier. I downed my drink in silence, then grabbed her hand and took her back to my room. If my marriage was ending, I was going to go out with a bang.

The next couple of weeks were long and miserable. Elvis had very little stamina and his shows were often embarrassing for all of us. He walked out on a couple of the shows, tossing his microphone down mid-performance and leaving the stage. Sometimes he returned after several minutes had passed, other times he did not. His uneven performances caused many reviewers to question, in print, whether the King of Rock 'n' Roll could still hold court.

Behind the scenes, frustration was building to a level that I hadn't imagined was possible. We knew that Elvis was in no condition to be performing, but we also knew that we couldn't cancel any more shows. Our job now was just to keep him alive and get him on stage. We returned to Baton Rouge at the end of May, making good on the promise to reschedule the show.

The tour lasted until June second, ending with a show in Mobile, Alabama. I knew that it was pointless to try calling Angie, because she was only going to hang up the moment she heard my voice. I figured I had a much better shot at getting her to give me one more chance if I talked to her in person.

She was already gone when I got back from the tour. I shouldn't have been surprised, but I was. Our apartment suddenly seemed so cold and empty without her there, and I knew that she had probably gone to Nashville to be with her family. As it turned out, I was right, and somehow I convinced Angie to come back to Memphis so that we could try to work things out. She was extremely reluctant but somehow she decided she'd give it a few more days. Elvis had been bothered by our split. He liked Angie and knew that she had been good for me. He wanted to see us work it out, mostly because he knew how upset I was that she'd left.

When he learned that Angie was staying with me for a few days, he summoned us to his room for a fatherly talk. We walked into his bedroom, where we found him wearing a long emerald-green robe over his pajamas. He was surrounded by Bibles and books about spiritual journeys, a subject that he had become increasingly obsessed with.

"Sit down, children, I want to talk to you," he said firmly, and I held back a laugh. Sometimes he took himself far too seriously, and I wondered what kind of marital advice he of all people could possibly have to offer. Elvis was cool, but sometimes he was just too far out there for me.

We sat down and Elvis made each of us give him one of our hands. He sat before us, his face earnest and concerned, asking if we loved each other. We both said yes. Elvis reached into the pocket of his bathrobe and produced his wedding ring. He handed it to Angie.

"I want you to have this," he said, as Angie stared back at him in shock. "This is a symbol to keep you together."

He began rambling on about marriage and relationships, and after several minutes he asked Angie to join him in the other room to speak with him privately. They left, and as I waited, I started thinking about what Elvis was like. The more I thought about it, the more livid I became. I knew that when it came to women, there was no boundary too extreme for him to cross. I would trust the guy with my life, but not with my wife.

I tried to stay within earshot to hear what they were saying, but all I could catch were vague, jumbled bits of words. By the time he rejoined me about ten minutes later, I was seething with anger.

"David, Angie will meet you downstairs in a few minutes," he said as he came back into his room and sat on the bed. "Now I wanna talk to you."

I looked straight at him and asked him the question that was burning through my heart and mind.

"Elvis, did you just try to do my wife?"

"What?" he asked, completely taken aback.

"Did you put the moves on Angie?"

He looked at me, still surprised, then broke into laughter.

"Well, no..." he answered.

"Well, you better not," I shot back, still mad. "That would not be a good idea."

"No! No – no – nothing like that," he said, obviously amused. "But I will tell you this, David – she's gone. She's not coming back to you."

I knew that I had no right to be upset; I had a woman in every town – sometimes more. Angie had been patient and tolerant for three years, and I had never given any indication that things would ever change. I couldn't expect her to live like that forever, but it didn't take away the pain. The other women didn't matter; they were just friends. They were women I had sex with to fill the empty hours on the road. Angie was different. She was the girl I loved, the one I came home to and shared a life with. I wished that I could find a way to make her understand that, but I knew that was both unfair and unreasonable.

Elvis could see how saddened I was by his words, and he put his arm around my shoulder and walked with me to the front window at Graceland. It was dark outside, and we could see the moon illuminating the ever-present throng of fans outside the gate.

"She's gone, David, but I just want you to remember one thing," he said, his voice taking on a wise tone. I looked at him expectantly, waiting to hear what bit of soothing wisdom he could impart on me.

"Somewhere out there, there's an eighteen-year-old shot of ass with your name on it."

I started laughing. It was typical Elvis logic, but most of all, I knew it was true.

Later, I would learn that Elvis had tried to convince Angie to come back to me, telling her that I really did love her.

"I don't think you guys know what love is," she countered. Looking back, I knew she was right.

Not surprisingly, Angie soon returned to Nashville and I began trying to pick up the pieces of my life without her. I would occasionally fly girls in to have them stay with me because I hated being alone. It felt like I had been alone until the day I met Angie, even though I was always surrounded by hordes of people. There was no such thing as doing something by yourself at Graceland – there were always people around and, for better or worse, you learned to appreciate the lack of solitude.

We were back on the road by mid-June and Elvis continued giving uncertain performances, looking pale and swollen. In Omaha on June nineteenth, 1976, his concert was recorded for a television special that would air later that year. For the next two nights, the concert was taped again and the footage from the second night wasn't even fit for broadcast. Although he did better on the third night, it definitely wasn't the same guy who had wowed crowds with his "Aloha from Hawaii" special. We all knew it. In just four years, he had undergone a shocking physical and mental transformation and the cameras were capturing it. We were tense as we watched him fumble his way through the shows, and relieved when it was over.

One of the last stops on the tour was at the Riverfront Coliseum in Cincinnati, Ohio. We had cordoned off the top floor of the hotel and were hanging out partying when Elvis suddenly appeared in my room. As we often did, all of us had our doors open so we could hang out together and move freely from one room to the next. Elvis rarely joined us these days, so I was surprised when he walked in wearing the now infamous black jacket with the DEA emblem.

"Let's go," he said.

"What?" I asked, not sure where we were going – or why.

"The air conditioner doesn't work," he said. "We're finding a different hotel."

Elvis' ballooning weight, coupled with the effect of the medications, made him always feel as if the room was ablaze. He kept his room at freezing temperatures, far below what the rest of us could tolerate. In this instance, he was unable to get the room cold enough.

Elvis and I got on the elevator, and I couldn't imagine how we were going to pull this off. I knew the lobby was filled with people, and I had no idea what hotel we were going to. He informed me there was another hotel across the street that we were going to check into. As we hit the ground floor, I took a deep breath and waited for the doors to open.

We walked out of the elevator and, for a brief moment, the crowd was frozen. No one expected to see Elvis simply stroll through the lobby. They stood shocked, unable to move. Ed Parker

253

and Dick Grob, happened to be in the lobby. As soon as they spotted us, they immediately rushed to Elvis' side.

We began walking across the street and it didn't take long for the crowd to follow. It must have been an unbelievable sight; the King of Rock 'n' Roll in a DEA jacket and his bodyguards racing across the street with a throng of screaming women at their heels.

I rushed into the first hotel I saw and asked if they had any rooms.

"We're full," the bored desk clerk told me. Just then, Elvis came bursting in behind me with Ed and Dick.

"You're not full," I informed the clerk. "This guy needs a room."

"Oh my god! It's Elvis!" he exclaimed, his eyes widening. "Yes sir, we'll find that room right away."

It was clear that we didn't have time to wait as the crowd poured into the lobby. Together, Ed, Dick and I hoisted him over the front desk and the clerk whisked him away to a back room, where he stayed until the hotel was able to secure a vacant – and well air-conditioned – room for him.

The tour ended the following night in Indianapolis. It was the best show we had seen him give in several months, and he stayed on the stage longer than usual. Still, for as well as he did, all of us were still troubled. We climbed aboard the *Lisa Marie* that night after the show and I sat next to Lamar, sipping a beer. His eyes were filled with worry and sadness as he watched Elvis make his way to the back of the plane.

"That boy," he told me sadly, "is not going to see the snow fly again."

I took a long pull on my beer and tried not to think about it.

We had almost six weeks until his next tour began, and we returned to Memphis exhausted. The sheer stress of getting Elvis on stage, of watching him every hour of the day and keeping him alive was wearing on all of us. When I wasn't working, I kept myself stoned or drunk or both, trying desperately not to feel the pain that was welling up within me. I couldn't stand to be in the empty apartment by myself, so I began staying with Shelly White and Aurelia Yarborough, a couple of Memphis hairdressers who sometimes cut Elvis' hair. I had become friends with them and it helped just to have someplace to go besides home.

Red and Sonny's book, called *Elvis: What Happened?* Was released on August first 1977 and the inevitable outcry began. Many fans refused to believe that Red and Sonny's accounts of life with Elvis were true; it seemed impossible that this icon could be a violent, unfaithful, emotionally troubled drug addict. Elvis was, of course, deeply bothered by it, and his conversations – regardless of the topic – often seemed to end up back on the book. He was alternately enraged and hurt; he talked about killing them one minute, only to begin crying and professing his love for them the next.

We didn't know what kind of fall-out we would see from the book, and knew that it wasn't until he went on tour again that we'd see whether or not the fans' loyalty was going to be affected by it. At any rate, it was going to be tough for him to get on stage, out of shape and slurring his words, without lending incredible credence to some of the accusations. We knew that any canceled shows, any problems with his performances, would be fodder for critics to point to Red and Sonny's book as a true account.

Nobody in our camp talked about the book, unless it was something Elvis brought up. Red and Sonny said the things that the rest of us knew to be true, things we had all thought ourselves at one time or another. In retrospect, the timing of the book's release would turn out to be terrible, but what they had to say was something that was bound to come out sooner or later.

Elvis talked about getting into a physical fitness regimen to get in shape for the next tour, which would begin in Portland on August seventeenth. However, his talk was mostly just that, as he continued to spend his days numbed out and often unconscious from the drugs in his three-times-a-day "Attack Packs." Much of my shift consisted of watching him sleep and making sure that he had assistance getting to the bathroom if he woke up since he was too drugged to make it there on his own.

That left plenty of time for me to talk with Ginger, who was only a year older than I was. I didn't have much in common with her other than our age and Elvis, but we talked about music and current events. She wasn't like Linda, who could motivate Elvis to do what he needed to do. Most of the guys felt like Ginger had the opposite effect on him. She didn't stay at Graceland like Linda or some of the other girls had, and that became a sore spot for Elvis as well. It seemed like she wasn't there when he needed her, making us all wonder how much longer they would really last.

Ginger introduced me to one of her friends, a pretty girl named Cindy, and I began dating her. It didn't make me long to give up on my relationship with Angie, and it helped me fill the hours when we were back in Memphis.

After a few mind-numbing and rather uneventful weeks, I decided to go to Nashville again and see Angie. I went to Elvis' room on August fourteenth and told him that I'd be back in time for the tour. He was in his room, reading the Bible, when I entered.

"Boss, I'm gonna head to Nashville for a coupla days," I told him.

He nodded knowingly. "You gonna try to fix it with Angie?"

I told him I was.

"I'm tellin' ya, David, she's gone," he said.

It didn't matter. I told him that I had to try. He nodded. I started to leave, but he stopped me.

"David, who am I?"

I looked at him, puzzled.

"What? You're the king!"

He lifted his Bible toward me and shook his head.

"Uh-uh – there's only one King."

I nodded, knowing there was no arguing with his spiritual musings.

"Come here, David."

I did as I was told, walking to his bedside. He opened his arms and pulled me into a big hug.

"I love you, David."

"I love you too, Elvis. Are you – um – is everything okay?"

He nodded, although his eyes misted over for a moment.

"I just wanted you to know that when you see me next, I'll be on a higher plane."

He motioned to his bedside table, which was littered with books on spiritual journeys.

"Sure, Elvis. The only plane I wanna see you on is the plane to Portland on the sixteenth."

He smiled and gave a little laugh.

"Alright, David. I'll see you on the sixteenth. Good luck in Nashville."

I began walking out the door and stopped. Something just wasn't right.

"Boss, are you – you sure you're okay?"

I turned to look at him, and he continued staring at his Bible, not returning my gaze.

"Goodbye, David."

I shut the door behind me. He was acting strangely, even by Elvis' standards. Maybe it was part of his growing tendency to be nicer to the people close to him, but he had seemed oddly affectionate. I pushed the questions from my head and went home to pack for my trip.

I drove to Nashville and tried in vain to get Angie to give me another chance. She had already met someone else, and I soon found out that she had begun seeing him while I was still on the road. For the first time, I understood Elvis' anger at Mike Stone when he started dating Priscilla. Just because I had cheated on my wife didn't mean that I didn't love her. I couldn't believe that while I was on the road, she had been in someone else's arms.

By the time I got back from Nashville I was tired, both physically and emotionally. I knew that getting back on the road was probably the best thing I could do. My marriage to Angie was beyond repair. Elvis had been right about that, she wasn't going to take me back. Now, even though I knew that in my head, it didn't keep me from wanting her back with all my heart. Or, with as much of my heart as I knew how to use at that time in my life.

Knocking on Heaven's Door

I returned to Memphis late on the fifteenth, where I was still staying with Shelly and Aurelia. My shift was scheduled to start around noon on August sixteenth, and I knew that it would be a couple of hours until Elvis would get out of bed. Shelly's brother, Mark, was staying with us, so I invited him to come along, knowing that we could shoot some pool or at least hang out until Elvis woke up.

My brother Ricky, Al Strada, and Joe Esposito were there when we arrived. Ricky said that when he had given Elvis his second Attack Pack earlier that morning, Elvis told him that he didn't want to be disturbed until around four o'clock.

"Is Ginger with him?" I asked.

Ricky nodded. We both knew what that meant-- he had someone watching over him, so our services weren't needed. Mark and I headed down the stairs, while Al Strada and Joe Esposito stayed upstairs in the jungle room preparing for our evening departure. About an hour later Ginger's ten-year-old niece, Amber, came downstairs with Lisa Marie. Lisa was staying with Elvis for two weeks, and Ginger had brought her brother's daughter to Graceland to give Lisa a playmate.

"David, Elvis is sick," the girls informed me.

"Who's with him?"

"Joe and Al are going up to see him now."

I looked at Mark, knowing my workday was just about to begin. "Let me run you home real quick," I told him. I turned back to Lisa Marie and told her I'd be back as soon as I took Mark home.

Mark and I walked into the house and Aurelia and Shelly looked at us, surprised to see us back so soon. We hadn't even spoken when I heard the first wail of an ambulance siren.

"Man, I gotta go. I gotta get back there," I said and began walking toward the door.

"What's wrong?" Aurelia asked.

I turned and looked at her. "Elvis is sick," I said

I hopped back into my 280-Z and turned onto Elvis Presley Boulevard. I could hear the ambulance sirens growing louder and, as I approached the gates of Graceland, an ambulance turned directly in front of me. My heart began to race. I knew something was different this time. It wasn't until then that I felt that this could be serious.

The ambulance followed the circular drive around to the front, while I took the other direction and drove directly to the back of the house. I ran into the house, but no one was downstairs. I knew they were probably all tending to Elvis, so I raced up the stairs to his room. I had just burst into the bedroom from one side when the paramedics pushed open the doors on the other side of the room.

I could see that everyone was in Elvis' bathroom; Joe, Al and Charlie were on the floor with Elvis and Vernon was leaning against the shower, supported by Sandy, his longtime girlfriend. I had never seen Vernon displaying so much emotion; he was moaning as if his heart were breaking.

"Don't die, son, please – don't die! No! Please!"

My gaze went to the floor, where Joe and Charlie had turned Elvis over. I stared in disbelief at my stepbrother. There was no question in my mind that he was already dead. His swollen tongue protruded from his mouth, his chest was bloated and blue and his eyes had rolled back in his head. I dropped down to his side and Vernon joined me. He took my hand and placed it on Elvis' cold, stiff leg.

"He's dead, David. My son is dead." Vernon moaned.

"What do we have here?" one of the paramedics asked.

"Drug overdose," I replied automatically. Joe and Al looked at me, shocked. I had just committed a cardinal sin amongst the inner circle– I had failed to protect the image of the man we were paid to keep safe at all costs. But it was the truth, and we all knew it. The paramedics rushed in and tried massaging his heart, but, unable to find any vital signs, they knew they had nothing to do but take him in to the hospital.

Suddenly, everything around me turned fuzzy. It seemed as everyone was moving in slow motion and each sound echoed hollow through my head. I looked at Vernon, who was consumed with grief. None of this seemed real.

"Get him on the stretcher!" I heard someone say, and I was vaguely aware of the body before me being moved. I looked around, dazed, and saw Attack Pack envelopes and pills on the bathroom floor. I noticed empty syringes, and the only emotion that was penetrating my shock was a dull sense of anger. Damn him! He had done this on purpose. I knew that now. He had known that when he told me good-bye two days earlier. How could he do this to us?

I began shoving the pills and envelopes into my pockets, knowing that they couldn't be left around for the police to find. This was still my job, at least for the moment, and I wasn't going to let him down.

"David!" Joe shouted at me. I heard my name, but it didn't really register. I just continued crawling around on the floor, grabbing pills off the floor.

"David! David, grab his legs and help us out here!" Joe yelled.

Still dazed, I walked over and reached beneath his pale green pajama pants to grab his ankles. As we lifted, I could tell that rigor mortis had set in. His skin was cool to the touch and his body was completely stiff. There was no way he was ever coming back home, at least not the way that we had remembered him.

We helped the paramedics carry him down the hallway, down the stairs, and to the waiting ambulance. We helped push the stretcher into the back of the ambulance, then Joe, Charlie and Al jumped in to join one of the paramedics, while the other paramedic climbed behind the steering wheel. I started to climb in as well, but just then Dr. Nick pulled up in his gold 450 Mercedes. As soon as I saw the doc, I stepped back and he climbed in.

The ambulance was now full, so I slammed the ambulance door and slapped it, signaling that they were good to go. The lights blurred with the wails of the siren as it sped down the driveway. I turned and ran back through the front door of Graceland, racing through the house and out the back door where I had left my car. Elvis' cousin, Billy Smith, who lived in a trailer on the property, was walking quickly toward the house.

"What's wrong?" he asked.

"Elvis is sick."

"What? What's wrong?"

"He's dead."

Billy stared at me, stunned.

"Get in the car, right now," I told him. "Let's go."

Billy quickly jumped in and I tore down the driveway, trying to catch up with the ambulance that was already long gone. As we reached the end of the driveway, Dick Grob and Sam Thompson were pulling in, blissfully unaware of what had just happened.

"Where you goin'?" Sam shouted out his window. He saw the look on my face and knew that something was up. "What's wrong?"

"Elvis is dead."

It was all I could say. I pushed the gas pedal to the floor and got to Baptist Memorial Hospital as fast as my car would let me go. We flashed our personnel cards at the hospital, and they led us to a room adjacent to the trauma room where the doctors were working on him. Dr. Nick was in the trauma room with the doctors, while Joe, Charlie, Al, Billy and I paced the floor and prayed for a miracle that we knew would never come.

I could hear the sounds echoing through my head; terse commands shouted over the sound of a ventilation machine, but I knew it was hopeless.

A doctor came in to check on us and Joe asked how long Elvis had been without oxygen.

"We don't know for sure, but it was quite awhile," the doctor replied. The truth of it all hit us like a ton of bricks. Even if they were somehow able to bring him back, he would be a brain-damaged shell of his former self. He had been found with his face buried in the bathroom carpet, and at that point, one belief was that he had suffocated.

"I guess we should hope that he's gone, then," Joe said, his voice trailing off. The doctor nodded sympathetically.

"That would probably be the merciful thing," he agreed.

We were tense and silent as the minutes ticked off the clock, and after about half an hour, which seemed to last forever, Dr. Nick came in and shook his head. We all knew it was over, but now Dr. Nick was squashing any bit of remaining illogical hope. From the moment we had walked into the bathroom, we had known he was dead. But this was Elvis, the larger-than-life man who seemed impervious to life's bullets, until someone told us point-blank that he was gone, there was really no way that we could believe it.

All of us stood there, stunned and dazed. We couldn't comprehend what had just happened, couldn't imagine what we had to do next.

"You have to tell the press." Dr. Nick said.

"Call a press conference," Joe replied.

I walked out of the hospital, confused and wracked with disbelief. Somehow I found my car and began driving back to Graceland. I reached down and turned on the radio, and the music was abruptly interrupted to make the announcement that Elvis Aaron Presley had been pronounced dead at the age of forty-two. The enormity and reality of the situation finally consumed me. I pulled my car to the side of the road and broke down into giant, chest-heaving sobs. It all hit me at once and I felt completely alone in the world. Elvis had been in my life for as long as I could remember and, for the past five years, I had put my service to him above everything else that I did—even my own life. I couldn't fathom a day without him, and it was impossible for me to picture my life without his presence.

I don't know how long I stayed on the side of the road, sobbing and swearing and drowning in pain and disbelief. By the time I got back to Graceland, Dr. Nick had already arrived from the hospital with the news. The scene there was nothing short of chaotic. Vernon's mother and Vernon were inconsolable, and everyone – Lisa Marie, Sandy, Amber, Ginger, Billy Smith and some of the other Presley relatives who lived at Graceland – were grief-stricken, alternating between sobs and numb stares. Ricky had returned to Graceland and we called our mother to give her the news. My brother Billy called to see if what he had heard was true. Fans already were beginning to gather at Graceland and the scene outside was as somber as it was inside. I couldn't take it. There was nothing left for me here, nothing for me to do. I numbly drove back to Shelly and Aurelia's house and gave them the news as I fired up a joint. I had no idea how I would make it through the next few days, let alone the rest of my life.

I didn't want to be around other people, so I went back to my old apartment, where my life with Angie was still a fresh, painful memory. I called Angie and told her that Elvis had died, but she had already heard the news on the radio. She promised me she would be there the next day. I wasn't involved in any of the arrangements. I just waited to get the phone call that told me where I needed to be and what I needed to do.

All that registered in my mind was shock. As surreal as the past seventeen years had been, this scenario beat everything I had seen during that time. I couldn't think about what this meant to me in terms of my life or what I would do the next day. Instead, I walked around shell-shocked, numbing whatever feelings that tried to bubble up with a bottle of scotch.

The next two days passed in a blur. Phone calls were made, and the media went into a frenzy as I watched it all separated by a thick glass wall of disbelief. I could see everything going on around me, could see myself functioning in this grieving world, but didn't feel as if I were still alive. Instead, I was just going through the motions.

We went on duty for the last time on August seventeenth, standing guard over Elvis' casket as thousands of fans paraded through the foyer to pay their last respects. More than 80,000 fans crowded outside of Graceland, though only 30,000 would be able to make it through the door. It was an unbelievable sight, with many fans fainting in the heat and others succumbing to their own grief. Through it all, we stood stoically in position, still taking care of business for the King of Rock 'n' Roll.

The gates had opened to mourning fans at three o'clock. Because of the incredibly large turnout, the planned two-hour public visitation went on until seven-thirty. When it was finally done, the coffin was moved back into the living room for the private service that was scheduled the next day. As hard as the day we'd just completed had been, we all knew that the tomorrow would be even tougher. I went back to the apartment with Angie and drank some scotch. Nothing seemed real.

We assembled at Graceland around noon the next day to get ready for the two o'clock service. Ginger's friend, Cindy, who I had been dating, came to my side, offering a hug and her sympathy. When Angie arrived just a few moments later, I again found myself in the awkward situation of having two women face off with one another. I hadn't told Angie that I was dating someone else, but it was obvious that Cindy and I were more than casual acquaintances. But we were all there for a much bigger reason, so nothing more was said about it.

There was a solemn sense of disbelief permeating the room, although Lamar did his best to keep all of us in good spirits. We were sitting on the back steps while visitors arrived for the service. We watched as Ann-Margret, Linda Thompson, and Priscilla exchanged condolences with one another. Lamar shook his head and gave a sly grin.

"I'll be damned," he said. "Leave it to Elvis to be able to get all those girls in one room without them clawing each other's eyeballs out."

We laughed. Lamar was right – I don't know any other man who could have pulled that one off.

About two hundred people attended the private ceremony. I sat on the wooden folding chair in a row that including Angie, my mom, Ricky and his girlfriend and Billy and his wife. Renowned preacher Rex Humbard and a minister named C.W. Bradley, who was the pastor at Whitehaven Church of Christ in Memphis, conducted the service, and J.D. Sumner and The Stamps sang hymns that they had been singing on stage with Elvis for many years.

Comedian Jackie Kahane wrapped up the service with a eulogy that was much less formal than what the ministers delivered. It was more representative of life on the road with Elvis, and it paid tribute to the sense of family that had been created by our time at his side. It wasn't until he said his final words – "Elvis has left the building for the last time" – that it all truly began to sink in. This was it. As surreal as it all seemed, it didn't get any more real than this. The life that I had known was over. If I hadn't been so numb, I would have wondered what I was going to do the next day, and the day after that. I would have wondered what I was going to do for a job, what I was going to do for money, what I was going to do with the rest of my life. But right then, none of that seemed important.

One by one, we filed past the coffin for one last look at the man who had been our leader but who had depended upon us so heavily, particularly in the past two years. I walked up with my mother and brothers and looked at the man who had welcomed me into his house seventeen years earlier. Despite what others said about him looking peaceful, I thought he looked horrible. Unfortunately, the Elvis that I had been dealing with the last few years was little more than a vacant, empty soul. I thought about my childhood at Graceland, of the indulgent Christmases, the extravagant vacations, the days spent on the back lots of movie studios while Elvis worked. A thousand memories flooded me, memories that began in my early childhood and now extended into life on the road at his side. It had been my job to be there for him, to protect him from whatever was out there that could cause him harm. Now, I wasn't sure what my role in life was.

I put my hand on top of his. His skin felt waxy and unnatural, and it struck me that I would never touch him, never see him, never talk to him again. I swallowed back the sobs that threatened to break free and continued on, allowing the remaining mourners to pass by. I watched as Priscilla and Lisa Marie filed by, then Vernon, who was completely broken, was escorted past his son's coffin. He had sobbed all the way through the ceremony, but saying a final good-bye almost proved to be too much. We stood at attention, not sure if he was going to physically be able to endure the grief of the moment.

When Vernon had finished paying his respects, the coffin was closed and the pallbearers – Joe Esposito, Charlie Hodge, Felton Jarvis, Lamar, Jerry Schilling, George Klein, Dr. Nick and Billy and Gene Smith – carried the steel-lined casket out the front door and down the steps of Graceland. I looked around as we walked out, knowing that my life would never be the same. This would be the last time I'd ever see Elvis, the last time I'd see many of these guys in the place we had all come to know as our home. I took Angie's hand and we walked down the steps to the waiting limousines.

Ginger had just walked out of Graceland when we heard a tremendous "snap" as the limb of one of the large oak trees broke off and fell, nearly hitting her. We all jumped aside, startled by the sudden activity and more then a little spooked. It was a living, healthy tree, and there was no visible reason for the limb to suddenly snap off like that.

I shot a look at Lamar.

"I think he's pissed," I joked.

Lamar grinned.

"We knew he'd be back, just not this soon," he quipped loudly.

We laughed. It was such a typically odd Elvis thing to have happen, as if he was letting us know that he was still around.

Vernon climbed into the first of sixteen white limousines with Lisa Marie, then the Stanleys – Dee, Ricky, Billy, myself – loaded into the second car along with our wives and Ricky's girlfriend. We were silent as we began the three-and-a-half-mile trek to the cemetery. I was stunned to see that the entire route was lined with mourning fans. Thousands of them lined the roads, and the image of them burned into my mind. I had spent the past five years watching people just like this, screaming or crying as they tried to get past me and get closer to the King of Rock 'n' Roll. They had often frustrated me, but now, as I watched them crying for a completely different reason, I realized just how much this one man had meant to them.

We arrived at the cemetery, making our way past an unbelievable assortment of floral arrangements. Fans sending flowers had exhausted the entire supply of flowers in Memphis, so reinforcements had been flown in from California to Colorado. In stark contrast to the brilliant colors was the simple, stark, gray mausoleum, which we entered silently. Rev. Bradley offered a few final words and then, one by one, we walked past the coffin one last time and back to the waiting limo.

That was it. We couldn't believe it was done. The world had lost an icon and I had lost a man whom I would never fully be able to explain. He was a stepbrother and a father figure; a best friend, yet a complete stranger. He angered me beyond belief, yet I loved him at all costs. I wasn't sure what any of that meant now.

Angie spent the night at our old apartment with me, then headed back to Nashville the following day. She hadn't been gone long when Vernon called and asked me to come over to his home on Dolan Street. It was the house I had grown up in, the same house that my mom lived in for about a year after she and Vernon separated. He now lived there with Sandy Miller.

I drove the familiar route that I had taken so many times, only now I felt a sense of heaviness as I drove past the famous gates of Graceland. Flowers and hand-made tributes were everywhere, and I looked away. I couldn't bear to see the memorials, couldn't stand to think about what had happened.

I pulled into the driveway of the house that once had been my home. I was weary, more tired than I'd ever felt before in my young life. As I entered the home I'd once shared with my mom and brothers, I found Vernon staring blankly at the wall. He looked horrible and I knew that he would never recover from this loss. This was the first time we had spoken since the day of Elvis' death, when I joined him on the bathroom floor.

"Vernon, I'm sorry," I began and he cut me off.

"I have to ask you something," he said curtly. His abrupt manner caught me by surprise.

"Oh – okay – what is it?"

"Did you kill my son?"

I couldn't believe what I was hearing.

"What?!"

He repeated his question, staring at me with cold, unfeeling eyes. As surreal as everything else had been over the past three days, this was too much. I couldn't even begin to understand what he was asking or where this was coming from.

"Daddy, why are you asking me that?"

"I spent several hours with Elvis the day before he died," Vernon said, his voice hoarse from sobbing. "The last thing that Elvis said to me before he died was, 'Watch out for David – I think him and Ginger have something going on.'"

He looked at me, accusingly, waiting for an answer. I could feel the rage beginning to rise inside of me.

"No, Daddy, I didn't."

The emotions of the past few days became too much. I broke down and began to cry, swearing to Vernon that there was nothing going on between Ginger and me. It was the truth. I knew better than to ever make a move on any of the girls Elvis brought around. Beyond that, I loved Elvis, and that was the one line that I would never have crossed. It broke my heart to think that Elvis might have had that suspicion, but I knew that, by the end of his life, the drugs were doing the thinking for him and had made him delusional. Vernon watched stoically as I sobbed, emotionally unable to reach out to me, but realizing that his suspicions were unfounded.

"Okay, it's alright," he said. "I'm sorry – I shouldn't have said anything."

He paused, knowing this wasn't the right time to say what he had to say, but also too consumed with his own grief to be too concerned with mine.

"Well, I guess your work here is done," he said, handing me an envelope with my final paycheck. "You take care of yourself."

At that moment, I realized that I had never been a son to Vernon, even though I called him Daddy, he never saw me as anything more than Dee's son. Billy, Ricky and myself were the baggage that came with my mother. I had been fortunate that Vernon had a son, someone who could step in, reach out and fill the role that I needed. Someone was there to care for me, and I had been truly blessed that Elvis was there to love me. Now that Elvis was gone, along with Dee, Vernon had no use for us boys. The only place we had in his life was in the past.

"You, take care of yourself, too," I answered and turned and walked out of the doors of my childhood home. It would be one of the last times I saw Vernon alive. A year and a half later I attended his funeral in the very room where Elvis' service was held. As quickly as I had been whisked into Graceland I was ejected from it. Life, as I had known it for the past seventeen years no longer existed.

Devastated by Vernon's words, I drove back to my apartment and sat alone, looking at what was left of my broken life. The biggest tragedy wasn't learning that the man I called Daddy had never reciprocated those feelings, the true tragedy for me was that the man who had first picked me up and welcomed me to his home was gone. I had watched as his chemical dependencies replaced the Elvis that I knew and loved, and by the end, I discovered that I both loved and hated him. I loved him for so many reasons, but I hated him for letting drugs destroy the man that I loved so dearly.

Eventually, I began to put the pieces of my life back together. I couldn't save my marriage, and it took awhile before I could even figure out how to save myself. I left Graceland with a ninth-grade education, an ample drug problem and a lot of wounds to lick. But once I was able to resolve each of those things, I was able to realize just how much I had.

It was simply fate that put me at the center of rock 'n' roll history. A chance meeting in a bar, a broken promise to my father--it could have been anyone else who lived the life that became mine. For whatever reason, fate chose to put me in the sidecar as Elvis blazed musical trails and created history. Elvis and I had a relationship that was due completely to circumstance. His father had an affair with my mother and married her. None of us had any say in it, and Elvis chose to make the best of it. He loved us and chose to help raise us, and eventually, we would return the favor by caring for him in similar accord.

Elvis had become so many things to me over the years. He was the guy whose shoes I wanted to fill, and whose shadow I could never evade. I lived to protect him, and would have given my life for him without a second thought. I protected him from the fans, from the media, from the real world, but in the end, I couldn't protect him from his worst enemy...himself.

Afterword

As I look back almost forty years after the death of the man I loved above all others, I am forever grateful to have been a part of his family. Elvis was bigger than life, and still is even in death. His accomplishments as an entertainer and dedication to his craft are unmatched to this day. He truly was, and still remains, the biggest entertainer of all time.

But beyond all the fame, fortune and hype, was a simple man who loved the Lord, his family, and his fans. A man who was haunted by demons and insecurities that plague us all, and eventually lost the battle of addiction, as too many often do. Elvis struggled with the dichotomies between who he really was and the image he was projecting, and could never find a way to align the two. This led to years of self doubt and depression that ultimately led to his death far too soon.

Because of my youth, I wasn't able to fully grasp what was happening, and was no match for Elvis in the throws of addiction. He was more the\an a King to me, he was my father figure, and I never thought a day would come where he wouldn't be there anymore. I had this naïve belief that Elvis could do anything— even overcome a prescription drug addiction. We had brought him back from the brink of death on more than one occasion, and I couldn't imagine a day where our best efforts would be in vain.

But that day did in fact come. On August 16, 1977 the world lost an icon, and I lost a brother. I hope that through the telling of this story, I can reach even one person struggling with addiction and save them from the same fate.

Elvis was the ultimate giver—he gave and gave until he had nothing left. In the years that followed his death, I would overcome the addictions that dominated my life, and took his. For me, his death became my resurrection, my wake up call to my road to redemption.

To Book David

A truly gifted speaker David's personal life story of triumph over adversity and stepping into his own greatness has impacted millions around the world. His powerful programs and contagious passion challenges and inspires individuals to embody the greatness of their personal selves.

David has been a frequent guest on Larry King Live, appeared on shows like 20/20, Good Morning America, The Today Show and CBS This Morning and has been the source of numerous articles for such publications as Life Magazine.

For more information on booking David E. Stanley visit:
WWW.DAVIDESTANLEY.COM
Phone: 858.256.4441 - E-mail: info@impelloentertainment.com

Help is Available

The cost of addiction today in the U.S. is a staggering $600 billion dollars, with over 15 million people abusing prescription drugs alone. David Stanley's intimate life story brings to light the struggles of the disease of addiction within a family who seemed to have it all.

As a Mental Health Professional, and addiction specialist for the past 30 years, I have worked with hundreds of people and their families in the recovery from substance abuse and addiction. For every person struggling, there are said to be at least 5 who are being significantly affected. What happened to Elvis Presley, and the effects it had on members of his family, continues to happen to millions of people worldwide today.

If you, or a loved one, are struggling with substance abuse and addiction, please take the step to ask for help now. Reach out to your local mental health care professional, who has the expertise and experience necessary to facilitate a successful recovery. You don't have to suffer in silence...hope and recovery is possible.

Sara G. Gilman, LMFT
Founder/President, Coherence Associates, Inc.
Licensed Marriage & Family Therapist
Fellow, American Academy of Experts in Traumatic Stress

To get help today for yourself or someone you love, call Coherence Associates at 760.942.8663.

To learn more contact:

Substance Abuse and Mental Health Services
http://www.samhsa.gov/find-help/national-helpline 1-800-662-
HELP (4357)

National Institute of Drug Abuse
https://www.drugabuse.gov/

Prescription Drug Abuse – Medline Plus
https://www.nlm.nih.gov/medlineplus/prescriptiondrugabuse.
html

CPSIA information can be obtained
at www.ICGtesting.com
Printed in the USA
LVOW03*0708101016

508095LV00005B/10/P

9 780996 666732